I'LL BE DAMNED

I'LL BE DAMNED
Goa

S N O P I X

Copyright © 2020 by SNOPIX.

ISBN: Softcover   978-1-6641-1227-8
              eBook   978-1-6641-1226-1

All rights reserved. No part of this book may be reproduced or transmitted in any form or by any means, electronic or mechanical, including photocopying, recording, or by any information storage and retrieval system, without permission in writing from the copyright owner.

Print information available on the last page.

Rev. date: 08/29/2020

To order additional copies of this book, contact:
Xlibris
UK TFN: 0800 0148620 (Toll Free inside the UK)
UK Local: 02036 956328 (+44 20 3695 6328 from outside the UK)
www.Xlibrispublishing.co.uk
Orders@Xlibrispublishing.co.uk

1

India, a distant, mystical land steeped in thousands of years of history. A place I never could have imagined travelling to before I met Steve, who gave me the chance to escape small-town Bournemouth on this adventure of a lifetime. We'd gotten as far as Athens, Greece, in the first part of this story, only to return to Amsterdam, or as I like to call it, "the Dam," where we spent most of the summer of 1976. I did get back to Bournemouth for a few days in July that year, to visit family and friends. Then, in late August, I headed to Switzerland to take a break, only to get myself arrested and spend the next four weeks fighting for my freedom which I did managed to achieve by some sort of miracle, and still seems like that today. However, you would already know this if you'd read the first part of *I'll Be Dammed: DAM* which is available at Amazon.

Anyway having gained my liberty from the Swiss, I was now determined to make the most of it by travelling farther than I'd ever gone before: India.

To be more specific, a small piece of tropical heaven, a state called Goa, situated about halfway down the west coast of the country. It is a paradise in every sense of the word, with silver sandy beaches, tall palm trees, and the pale-blue waters of the Arabian Sea lapping its shore. This now became the focus of the second part of my story; this journey took me through some of the most barren, inhospitable landscapes I'd ever seen.

First would be Turkey, then Iran, Afghanistan, and Pakistan, which were all very similar, with what felt like endless dusty plains punctuated by hills and mountains along the way. The temperatures went from extremely hot during the day—in fact, hotter than I'd ever experienced—to freezing cold at night.

When we reached the Pakistan-India border, I beheld a sight that would humble anybody. I had thought the Alps were impressive until I saw the majesty of the Himalayas, a sight that surpassed the Alps in every way and left me full of wonder about our vast, amazing planet. In the shadow of that mighty mountain range were the lush, green jungles and forests of northern India, the complete opposite of all those inhospitable, barren plains. It was really a journey of enlightenment for me. However, here I am, many miles down the road already, when I should be telling you what happened in the Dam as I prepared to leave one more time.

2

Leaving was something I was getting used to now, after being stuck in Bournemouth for most of my life. So, with only my bag to pack, I'd be ready to go. However, there was one thing still missing: my drawings, which I still couldn't find. I had to accept they were gone forever, never to be seen again. Steve, John, and Don had done all the preparations to get the coach ready, as venturing out on such a long journey without thoroughly checking it over first would be ill-advised. We took some spares like airbags for the suspension and at least two spare tyres, because once you got past northern Turkey, the quality of the roads became very dubious; a lot of them turned into little more than dirt tracks full of potholes. So the last thing you needed was an airbag or a tyre to blow, as there wasn't exactly an AA man to call—or even a telephone box to call him from on the roads we would soon be travelling on. So if you did get stuck in the middle of nowhere without any spares, you were f**ked.

According to John, spares were available in the larger cities, but that wouldn't help if you were stuck on a desolate road in the middle of nowhere. You'd only have the occasional donkey to hitch a ride on, if you were lucky enough that one was passing. It was good to have John's experience to draw on; having him along for the journey would come in very handy if anything went wrong with the coach (and it did).

Something else that was essential for a smooth journey was some bottles of scotch whiskey and cartons of Western cigarettes. These were used as bargaining tools to help ease our way across the borders we were now heading for. A bottle or carton put in the hand of the right customs guard meant you would have no problems getting through. Another good thing to take were all types of Western goods, particularly Levi's jeans, which were very sought after and worth a lot of money in these Eastern countries. Time was also of the essence now, because the guys had waited, just in case I did get back. It was already the first week of October, so we needed to leave soon. We were going to the mountains in northern Greece and Turkey, which we needed to get through before the end of October. After that, the roads became impassable because of snow and ice, so we'd be going nowhere.

So we talked to the Magic Bus guys, and they scheduled us to be the last coach leaving the Dam on the twelfth, which was in five days. That would leave us just enough time to get through, we hoped.

3

Ready—with all the journey's preparations done and the date set to leave, we were. There was only one thing left now, the thing we all loved to do most, which was to have a leaving party to send us off in style. So where did I find myself again? The Inside Out Club, of course, buck naked on stage, f★★king Eve's brains out, completely off my head. This was a night I did remember. The days leading up to our departure were filled with a lot of drug-taking and a lot of sex, as much as I could get, because it would be the last time I'd see Eve. I did ask her to come with me, but she wasn't ready to leave the Dam just yet. So we made the most of our last few days together, by her taking time off work and us never leaving each other's side. She was the only thing that made me think about staying, because I think I was in love—or was it just that beautiful body I didn't want to leave? Well, in the end, my wanderlust got the better of my sexual lust, as the pull of the road was just too strong.

Leaving was hard, though. I asked her not to come to see the coach off, preferring to leave her lying in bed with the memory of our last night together.

But that morning, she insisted, saying, "It's probably the last time we'll see each other anyway, so let's have every last minute."

How could I say no to that? I don't think I'd ever gotten so close to someone in such a short time and under such strange circumstances—then or ever again.

The departure time that morning was at twelve, so it was back to the boat to get my bag and say my good-byes to Eric and Frank. I found no one on board, just a note on the door telling me to get my arse to the Magic Bus office as soon as I'd read it. So that's where we headed, and what a sight it was. We turned the corner to witness a throng of what must have been a hundred people all surrounding the office and coach. Only twenty of those were actually passengers, who were all seated on the coach, looking quite bemused by what was going on around them. So, it seemed, were the Magic Bus guys, who had never seen a departure quite like this before. They thought it was probably down to Don and Gary, the man from the first part of my story, who'd given me my first tab of LSD, joining us on our trip.

It all had a party feel to it, only this time, not at the Inside Out Club, but on the street, with Eric and Frank there cheering away. Somehow, all this commotion helped to make the leaving process easier to deal with for both Eve and me, but there were still some tears on both our parts. When we finally did get underway, it felt like some sort of parade, with all the cars around us sounding their horns. All that was missing was the ticker tape and a banner saying "Have a good trip" or "Next stop, India."

4

Sweep the last passenger up along the way. That's what the last Magic Bus to India did, so that's exactly what we did. This meant our first stop would be Brussels to pick up four and then Athens for another six. Only this time, finding the Brussels train station wasn't a problem with John driving. He knew all the shortcuts, so we were there in no time. With those passengers on board, we were heading for Germany, which is the fastest way south towards Athens. This was also the first time Don and I had been any real distance in this coach, and like Steve said before, it was a dream to drive and ride in. So we sat back to enjoy Europe passing by the window. When we did cross the German border, I could only think of the last time we'd done this route and laugh with Steve about how rubbish our first bus had been.

What a difference it was this time as we cruised down the autobahns with hardly a sound from the engine, just the whistle of the wind passing over the coach we were travelling in. As we touched 100 kpm, Mannheim, Stuttgart, and Munich seemed to fly by in this amazing time machine of a coach. Then avoiding Switzerland for obvious reasons, we were into Austria and those breathtaking views of the Alps, with their deep beautiful alpine valleys. Yugoslavia came next as we headed for Zagreb and Belgrade, with its drab austere architecture and sprawling rundown suburbia, which were mainly tenement blocks. If this was a true reflection of communism, it wasn't much of a dream; more like a concrete nightmare. We made the mistake of stopping for supplies at what looked like a supermarket, only to find that all the shelves were empty apart from one, which had jars of pickles, bread, and potatoes on it. That all there was for sale.

It was such a contrast to the beautiful medieval architecture of the towns and cities on the coast road. We didn't stop for supplies on that trip, so I can't comment on what was available in the shops there. There wasn't time for the serpentine coastal road, with its high cliffs that took us above the clouds and the amazing views of the Adriatic Sea. As we needed to get to Athens ASAP.

On my first visit to ancient Athens, there had been time to do some sightseeing, with us ending up at Brad's Bar near the beautiful Greek island of Poros, where I celebrated my twentieth birthday. This time, only a few short months later, I was like a different person due to my Swiss jail experience; I felt like I'd aged ten years or more from what had happened to me in the Dam over the summer.

Now, though, it was straight to the Magic Bus office, where our last passengers were waiting. Two of these were Liza and Lucy, both attractive, precocious Americans. Who instead of just sitting back to enjoy the journey, they later became part of the story too through their own precociousness. After they were safely on board, we departed, with no great leaving party like in the Dam, just the need for speed to beat the weather. We managed to get there just in time. So now we could just cruise to our next stop, Istanbul.

5

The border from Greece into Turkey is where everything slowed down, because even after bribing the main guard with a bottle of scotch, he still insisted on checking everybody's passport, so there we sat for a good two hours while he went through everything, including the papers for the coach (which I'm happy to say were all in order). We were then on our way again, and even though visually there was little difference to Greece, I did feel that crossing the border was a giant leap for me, as the world shifted from west to east, so there was no turning back now.

We now headed for the sea of Marmara, then following its northern coastline around until Turkey's most famous city, Istanbul, came into view. What a sight it was, with the vast blue mosque dominating its skyline. Now I thought Athens was a mess until I saw Istanbul, which looked like a vast warren of mud huts from a distance, all interspersed with the turrets of more mosques. It was the most in-your-face city experience in my life to that point, but that would change later in the journey. The closer we got to the city centre, the worse the traffic got, until it was just a big traffic jam, with an occasional lurch forward, which you had to be ready for.

Otherwise, some quick-witted driver in another vehicle would dive into the place and the rest of the traffic would close up, so you'd go nowhere fast.

This was when I first experienced the great Eastern practise of bringing the market to you, because while the coach was held up in all this traffic, we were surrounded by people trying to sell us anything from snakes and goats to chickens, even a guy trying to sell us his children (at least that's what I thought). It was quite something to behold as more sellers clambered over cars or squeezed through gaps with carpets, bags, pipes, or anything else they thought we might buy. For the people living there, the sight of a Western coach was like a gift from above, because if they did manage to sell you something, it was for far more than they'd ever get if they sold it to a local, with you thinking you got it cheap.

Another first for me was the great Eastern art of haggling, which again was something to behold when you watch two masters at it, like John and Gary, who from all their time spent in the East had become very adept at it. I did pick up some good tips from them, before first trying it myself. Only I didn't have their determination and desire to go on for as long as it took. I would give in too easily, because even at the price I was paying, it was still cheap to me. Later on this journey, after I'd had more practise, my haggling skills improved immensely.

However, the main reason we were stuck in this traffic jam, instead of taking the roads around the city, was the need to get high, or to put it more bluntly, to buy drugs.

6

Opium was something we all wanted; well, most of us on the coach, anyway, especially Don, who'd only brought a small amount of heroin with him from the Dam, because of the borders in Europe. Now he needed fresh supplies and was very grateful Gary was with us, because he knew just where to get the stuff. This is why we were stuck in this traffic jam from hell, going nowhere fast. However, we eventually got through to where we wanted to go, which was the main market in the centre of the city.

After the coach stopped outside, the noise from the market took over, although there was still some from the traffic. Now, though, it was mainly from the many people shouting at each other, haggling, of course. Then as Gary, Don, and I left the confines of our lovely air-conditioned coach to go on our quest for opium, we were hit by the smells that also came into play. They were of incense and spices infused with what I could only think was human and animal sweat, from all the livestock and unwashed human bodies. There were also some open sewers in close proximity, with who knows what in them., to add to the final je ne sais quoi of it all. The combination of the noise and all these aromas made my senses tingle inside and out, as we headed into this maze of tunnels made up of market stalls, or souk stalls, to give them the local name.

Both Tom and I were more than happy to let Gary lead the way, because after a just short distance walking into this maze of tunnels, we would have been lost. Our progress was also slowed by every stallholder thrusting his wares in front of us as we tried to negotiate our way though, making it more like a fight at times; we were being offered so much. Everything from Persian rugs to live snakes were laid before us.

We finally got to the stall Gary was looking for; we stepped off the main thoroughfare into what looked like just another bag and rug stall. We were then greeted by a small smiling man dressed in Arab robes; he and Gary bowed, shook hands, and passed some words. Then we were ushered behind a carpeted wall only to find a large tented room, that turned out to be an opium den, which made sense, of course. All the noise of the souk was gone now; what replaced it was this strange melodic wailing of a man playing a flute-like instrument in the far corner.

After a few moments, my eyes adjusted to the lower light, and more people came into view. They were lying on large cushions scattered around the place, and seemed to be either enjoying their opium buzz or being tended to by helpers, who loaded and lit their opium pipes. We were then greeted by another smiling man, who indicated for us to sit; he seemed to know Gary too, as they bowed to each other and shook hands. Then after some more words were passed, the smiling man disappeared, and Gary joined us on the cushions.

"Okay," he said. "I've ordered us a pipe each for now and a kilo of opium and hash to go."

We were then joined by the smiling helpers, who surrounded us and showed us where to lie down before handing us our pipes. They then held a flame to the pipe's bowl to ignite the opium. I'm not sure what happened after I inhaled deeply on my pipe, but was very glad I was lying down, because my whole body and mind turned instantly to jelly, like all the bones, including my scull, had been removed.

My helper saw this and managed to catch the pipe as it fell from my hands. He'd obviously seen this before, because he just laid it on the floor in front of me and left with a smile. Or that's what I think happened, because this was like no opium buzz I'd ever had in the Dam. The whole room started to spin around my head like a giant washing machine, with all the smiling faces swirling around me. Then I started to fall into a bottomless black abyss of silence, as all the sounds around me disappeared too. It was hard to tell how long this lasted before I heard Don's voice, faintly at first, then slowly growing louder as sound and light did return, and I came back to the reality that surrounded me.

He was asking, "Are you okay? We thought we'd lost you there."

After I finally found my way out of that deep black hole, I managed to say, "Wow, what a rush that was."

"I forgot to say you should take it easy with the opium here," Gary said, "because of its freshness. It's much stronger than anything you'd get in the Dam."

I'd had some mind-blowing drug experiences over the summer, but this had to be one of the strangest, almost like I died and came back to life again, as if I knew what that was like in the first place. I think the true reality was, I came very close to overdosing, the opium was so strong here.

"And there I was, thinking I could handle my drugs," I added.

Don said, "It could happen to anybody who doesn't know the strength of opium they're dealing with."

I was still floating as we were treated to a repeat performance by the stallholders as we made our way back to the coach. Steve was laughing at me as Gary and Don helped me up the coach steps, saying, "He's okay, just took too big a hit of opium."

Later, after I regained my senses, I asked Gary about all the cloak and dagger at the opium den.

"Even though Turkey produces the drug," he explained, "it's still illegal to take them, even for the Turks, but a lot worse for Westerners, especially if they're caught trying to take them out of the country."

That was exactly what we intended to do next. So a good place to stash them was needed, and John knew just the spot: a compartment at the back of the engine bay that had a hidden catch and looked like a part of the body work. It was usually used for tools and now made the perfect hiding place, with the added bonus of the smell of the engine oil covering the pungent aroma of the drugs.

It turned out the hash we bought was just as good quality as the opium, because it laid to waste everybody on the coach who tried it. Now with the drug situation sorted, next we needed to get fresh supplies of food and water. Then it was on to a garage John knew on the outskirts of the city to check the bus over and fill up with diesel. We now had everything needed in order to take our next giant step, onwards to Iran.

So with everything checked and our new stock of drugs well stashed away, and with food and water to last several days on board, we watched Istanbul and Western Europe disappearing in the rear-view window. Eastern Asia now opened its arms to welcome us in, with the promise of a whole new adventure.

7

The choice of how to cross Turkey came next, as we left the confines of Istanbul and headed out into what looked like an endless desert, apart from the road, that is. After consulting the map, because we had one this time, we could either take the main road through the centre of the country or the coast road. This would take us along south shore of the Black Sea towards Trabzon. So we put it to the passengers and found ourselves heading for the coast. This wasn't as dramatic as the Adriatic coastline, with its serpentine road and high cliffs. It was more reminiscent of the Gulf of Corinth in Greece, with a biblical feel of small fishing villages and boats along the shore, but still worth the extra time it took rather than driving the main route.

The Black Sea was a beautiful backdrop as we followed along its shoreline, through Zonguldak and Samsun, quite a large city with a long history, going back to 750 BC, when it was called Amisos. After consulting the map again and talking to Gary about the region, I began to learn about the history of the part of the world we were passing through, which is reputed to be the cradle of civilisation where the first signs of organized towns and cities have been found.

That will teach me for not paying attention in history and geography lessons at school (or even going to school in the first place, as I bunked off most of my senior year).

When we did reach Trabzon, this beautiful ancient city came into view, with more mosques and a variety of architecture like Istanbul, only not on the same scale. The place had a stunning setting as well, in the lee of the eastern Black Sea mountains. Trabzon's history went back many thousands of years, when it was part of the Silk Road. Its Black Sea port connected it to the outside world then, and it still does, although there's also an airport as well now.

This is where we left the Black Sea behind us to head inland towards the Zigana Pass, another famous landmark in the area, for its access to the Armenian frontier going north and Iran going south. We were heading south to a place called Dogubeyazit, near the Iranian border.

8

Crossing the Iranian border could be a bit tricky, according to John. Even though the shah, who was in power at the time, had been trying to bring the country into the twentieth century, because of its size, that only really affected the capital, Tehran. The rest of the country remained well and truly stuck in the past, which wasn't such a problem for the men, but for Western women, it was, which was how our two precocious Americans, Liza and Lucy, came into the story.

First, though, we had to negotiate the Turkish side of the border, which looked very imposing as we drove up, all barbed wire, guard dogs, and armed soldiers. Plus we were now leaving the country with the drugs, which made us nervous, only just as we were about to stop at the gate, the guard lifted it and waved us through. This was lucky because, according to John, using alcohol or cigarettes as a bribe was unpredictable with the Turks, who were Muslim. So you couldn't be sure how they might react. Some of the guards would be okay and accept it, while others could take offence, then you could be stuck there for hours trying to get through. That was what happened when we entered the country, only we didn't have the drugs then. This whole smuggling thing that Gary mentioned before, and with us being in a Western-registered coach, usually those two things were put together, and we'd be stopped. Only not this time, thank heavens, as we passed through with no problems.

No such luck on the Iranian side, as we were flagged down. This was when a bottle of scotch did work, because just as it looked like the guard was going to check every passport, John, who'd been across this border many times, was recognised by one of the guards; they smiled and shook hands. Then after a few words were exchanged, John deftly passed the bottle to the guards, and there was no passport check. The gate was lifted, and we were through. It had all taken no longer than ten minutes, and everybody on board was very happy we had John with us, so when we were well clear of the border post, all the passengers started shouting his name.

Once we were in Iran, it felt like we gone back further in time, as it had an almost prehistoric feel to it, compared to the biblical feel of Turkey. However, unlike Turkey, there wasn't a choice of routes, so no sea views to ease our way this time. Just one main road through the centre of the country, with the very occasional side road running off it.

Now it was on to Tabriz, which apparently was the fourth-largest city in Iran; it was the capital some two thousand years ago. It was also known for having the largest covered bazaar in the world, and what was mainly sold there? Yes, you guess it: carpets.

We drove right through Tabriz; we had no choice, as the concept of ring roads or bypasses hadn't reached this part of Iran yet. It was like we'd landed on another planet; it made me think of the coach being a time machine going backwards. It was the first sign of any real life we'd seen after driving from Turkey across what felt like a vast endless plain, with only the occasional crop of rocky cliffs, and not a soul to be seen. It really felt like we'd left the earth and were on the moon; it was so desolate. Once we were past Tabriz, there were some more signs of life with people, goats, and the occasional village passing us by. So it didn't feel like it was quite so barren like before.

We were now heading for Tehran, which we all know as the capital of Iran and by far the largest city we'd seen since Istanbul. First, though, there was Zanjan, with, yes, you guessed it, another locally famous bazaar selling even more carpets, but nowhere near on the scale of the one in Tabriz. Next came Qazvin, which apparently was well known for the tomb of Shardeh Hoseyn, one of Iran's famous rulers from the past. Then with the Elburz Mountains to our left, sheltering us from and restricting our view of the Caspian Sea, which lay beyond them, we approached Tehran, where we had our first problem with the coach.

9

Leak in the airbag on the right-hand rear suspension. That's what our first problem turned out to be, only it didn't stop us; it just slowed our progress until we could find some solid ground to work on. This was where Liza and Lucy came into the story. Up until then, although a bit loud at time, they were quite overwhelmed by the amazing scenery we were travelling through, like most of the other passengers. However, that hadn't stopped all the boys on board, including myself, trying to get in their pants (with no success, I might add).

So as we came into the city, we were looking for a garage of some sort where we could work on the coach. What we needed was some solid ground where the coach's body could be jacked up and supported, then the new airbag fitted. Eventually, we managed to find a lorry park with a workshop where we could do the repairs, that is, after giving these two dodgy-looking guys who ran the place a pack of cigarettes each.

The work, as long as there were no problems, would take about an hour, according to John, but all the passengers had to disembark so the coach could be jacked up. Most of them went for a wander around the local area, only it wasn't long before we heard screaming and shouting coming from behind the workshop. Dropping our tools, John, Steve, Don, and I all ran towards the noise, getting there just in time, because there were Liza and Lucy, surrounded by a gaggle of local men, including the workshop owners, who all obviously had one thing on their minds, which was sex with them.

The girls were only dressed in skimpy tee shirts and shorts because of the heat, so they might as well have been naked to these guys. The women in Iran were rarely allowed out of their house and had to be completely covered, from head to toe, including a mask over their face. So with Liza and Lucy dressed the way they were, it was like a red flag to a bull to these guys. Luckily, most of the other passengers heard the commotion and came running too. So through weight of numbers, we managed to get between the girls and their potential assailants to calm the situation and then get them back to the coach.

After that, we managed to change the airbag in record time, according to John, and then hightailed it out of that place before anything else could happen. That experience had quite an effect on Liza and Lucy, because from then on, not only did they cover themselves when they left the bus, they were also much friendlier to everybody who helped rescue them, giving all the boys more of a chance to get into their pants, including myself, with some success later on this journey.

10

Tehran, the city itself, looked very impressive set against the Elburz Mountains as we drove in. It was by far the most cosmopolitan place we'd seen so far on our journey (well, the centre, anyway). Its eclectic mix of modern Western and ancient Eastern architecture made the experience quite surreal. All this modernisation was down to the shah who, with an endless quantity of oil money and the help of the Americans, was trying to drag the country out of the Stone Age and into the twentieth century. Only a few years after we were there, he was overthrown by a revolution in the country, which was mainly down to him spending most of the oil money on himself, his family, and his mates.

However, as a contrast to all the modernisation the shah was doing and to show just how old the city actually was, the Grand Bazaar in the southern part of the city had been on the same site for over eight thousand years. Now, that is real history, which was where the shah's main problems lay; it's easy to use money to change a place's facade, but changing the fundamental culture of a society is something money can't do by itself. That can only be done by time, money, and most importantly the will of the people. From what I could see just driving around the place, and having witnessed the attitude of the guys who'd tried to assault Liza and Lucy, this was still a long way off. Living in a country where the ancient and the modern coexist in such extremes, there's always going to be conflict. So progress is never going to be easy, and it's always going to be a fight to make any real change.

As we drove through the centre of the city, it was like a modern oasis compared the urban sprawl of its suburbia. In some ways, this wasn't much different from most cities in the West. The main difference was in the mindset of the people and the way they were dressed, wearing Eastern-style clothes, rather than jeans, tee shirts, or suits.

Now, as we left another surreal experience behind, we were about halfway across Iran and were getting closer to the country all consumers of fine cannabis resin would like to visit at least once in their lives: the legendary Afghanistan.

11

Afghani Black is one of the finest hashes in the world, and just the mention of its name would have any dope smoker in the West saying how they'd love to try it or eulogising about their experience smoking the stuff and how the high attained from this legendry hash was almost spiritual. Even though they couldn't be sure it did actually come from the place, because there wasn't exactly a bill of sale or certificate proving it did. And there were similar hashes from other parts of the world, which were almost as good, so you could never be sure.

Only now, with the country of its origin almost within touching distance, that was all about to change for me and most of the other passengers on the coach who wanted to try it, because we were about to sample the real McCoy. That's as long as they let us into the country, of course.

There were no problems at both the border out of Iran and into Afghanistan, with John placing the bottle of scotch or carton of cigarettes in the right guard's hand, and again, we all gave thanks and praise for him being with us. After we were through, we first headed for Herat, then it would be on to Kabul, the capital, but like in Turkey, there was another choice of roads we could take. Only this time, there was no sea road to entertain us. There was a route through the centre of the country, which would take us through the mountains, or we could go around them to the south through Kandahar, which was longer but much safer. I say safer, because according to John, the mountain road was quite spectacular but much more precarious due to snow and rock slides that could happen at any time and slow our progress, hit us, or block our way completely. There was also a third route to the north, but we didn't consider that because when we again put it to the vote, everybody on board wanted to go through the mountains.

This turned out to be even more impressive than the coast road in Yugoslavia, only this time without the Adriatic Sea. Instead, there were breathtaking views of endless mountain ranges, with what looked like bottomless green ravines between them. Luck also seemed to be on our side, as we managed to negotiate this very dangerous road without any real difficulties or mechanical problems. In the end, though, it did take longer than we anticipated, because a lot of it had to be driven very slowly. There was ice on the road and no crash barriers to stop us plunging into one of those deep green ravines.

However, seeing Kabul as we came down from this mountain road, set in the Panjshir Valley in the lee of the Hindu Kush mountain range, made that sight alone worth the extra time. Tehran had a similar setting but was nowhere near the same size, mainly because it didn't have the modern oasis in the centre, but it looked just as impressive. Banners and flags flew from a lot of its buildings, beautifully set at the bottom of the valley, against those very impressive mountains.

12

Plan: It was on this leg of the journey that I found out that there was one; we weren't visiting Kabul just to find real Afghani black hash and experience the city. No, there was a much bigger scheme behind this visit, hatched while I was incarcerated in Switzerland but only conveyed to me now. The plan was to smuggle as much Afghani cannabis and opium that could be comfortably stashed in the coach. The plan was to go first to Pakistan and then on to India, where there was still a good profit to be made, as long as it was top-quality stuff. This deal had been instigated by Gary, who'd done it before and had no trouble selling the idea to Don, Steve, and John. He had a contact in Kabul to buy the stuff from and a buyer first in Ahmadabad, who would take half the load. Then the rest would be taken farther on to Goa and sold there. Only there was one fly in the ointment: it was still very illegal in these countries, where the stuff was made, to move hash and opium across borders.

Anyway, the passengers were dropped off at a hostel Gary knew in the centre of Kabul to spend a few days exploring the city, while Gary, John, Steve, Don, and I went in search of Gary's contact, Nadir. We found him in a tea shop not far from the hostel, where he was smoking tobacco (I think) from a hookah-style pipe. He looked like he was in his midthirties, only it was hard to tell, with his weather-beaten leathery skin and narrow piercing eyes that I'm sure had seen many a harsh time in this extreme part of the world. He looked like a real character too, dressed in tribal robes with a rifle slung over his shoulder and dagger sheathed across his chest.

Also, when he did smile, he had this toothy grin, and a glint came into his eye, making you wonder if he was actually friendly or about to slit your throat. However, what did give him an edge was being able to speak fairly good English, which he used to great effect to further his business interests. He now used it to play middleman, directing us north out of the city towards a farm near Doshi, which was situated in those Hindu Kush mountains.

What a sight to behold, and there I was thinking the Alps were impressive, that is, until I saw the majesty of the Hindu Kush close up. It was almost incomprehensible the size of the wilderness laid out before my eyes, and something to humble anybody who witnessed it. Just range after range of peaks that seemed to have no end, and all connected up to the mighty Himalayas. This was the view from the farm we were taken to, although I'm not sure if you'd really call it a farm, because it was just a collection of ramshackled buildings in the middle of nowhere.

We were greeted by the smiling farmer and his family, who welcomed us into their home. The buildings may have looked decrepit from the outside, but inside, they were warm and snug and lined with beautiful carpets and elaborately decorated cushions. This helped to keep out the winter's cold temperatures and winds on this high plateau. If we'd come a few weeks later, it would have been inaccessible because of the weather, so our timing was just right again. Even now, though, I didn't linger too long looking at the view because it was already getting cold outside. I was starting to understand why so many carpets and cushions were sold at the souks and bazaars. They were used for insulation.

The Afghan family were very friendly and couldn't do enough to make us feel at home, sharing everything with us over the next two days, while we did the deal and stashed the hash and opium in the coach. We never did get to know them that well, only really dealing with the farmer himself, who like Nadir had that wild, untamed look, but without the rifle and dagger. We only saw his wife and children when we arrived, when they brought us food, and when they waved goodbye as we left. The deal itself took up the first day and involved drinking this hooch the farmer made himself, a very strong concoction made mainly from fermented goat's milk, according to Nadir, who couldn't get enough of the stuff. The farmer was very proud of his hooch and let out this strange cackle of a laugh at the faces we pulled when we drank it the first time. We were then treated to a sight almost as good as the Hindu Kush mountains, as we were taken to one of the other buildings, and the doors were opened to reveal the most cannabis and opium I'd ever seen in one place. These were the farmer's summer crops, and he was very proud of them too.

So now came the deal, because it wasn't as simple as just trying it and buying it. No, now it was how much money did we want to spend, which would then determine what quality of hash we'd get and, therefore, how much hash we'd get for the money. This wasn't the case with the opium, which only came in one grade: mind-blowing. With the hash, there were three grades, but that didn't include the very best, which the farmer kept for himself.

So the sampling began, and yes, finally, here I was, actually smoking Afghani black hash in Afghanistan.

We worked our way through each of the grades, with the first one being reminiscent of what was smoked in the West, which any dope smoker in their right mind would have happily settled for. Only now we had two more grades to go, and they did exactly what you'd expect by getting us more and more stoned. I thought I was doing okay the more out of it I got. However, it was the last thing on the menu that got me again, and that was, you guessed it, the opium.

I thought I'd learnt from Istanbul not to inhale too deeply on the pipe, but this opium, because it was even fresher than then, was even better. So I soon found myself again disappearing into that black endless abyss. Only this time, I found myself in a strange opiate dream. But when I awoke the following morning, lying on the warm carpet wrapped in a blanket, it disappeared from my memory like the rest of that night.

"Hope I didn't make a fool of myself," I said, when I finally came around and managed to unglue my tongue, which was stuck firmly to the roof of my mouth. Yuk.

"So you are alive," Don said, laughing at me. "We thought we'd lost you again."

The farmer was also cackling at me, saying something incomprehensible, which Nadir translated to calling me a "lightweight," or words to that effect.

So I laughed along with him, then the farmer cheered and hugged me as I stood up and took big drink of his goat's milk hooch, which tasted even more disgusting than I remembered, but certainly woke me up.

We spent the morning of second day hiding the drugs in the coach, which didn't take that long, because John knew just what to do, as he'd used this space before. This time, it was under the seats. First, you had to take the padded part off by pulling it towards you and lifting. This revealed a holding tray, where you could easily fit ten plaques of opium or hash, which we brought the best grade of. So working from the back of the coach, we loaded every seat, half of them with hash and the rest with opium. Then the money exchanged hands, with Nadir getting a cut for his part in the deal, making everybody involved more than happy. We then said our goodbyes to our very friendly hosts for those two days, and with one last look at those magnificent mountains, we were on our way again.

Now we had a decision to make, which was what to tell the passengers. When we got back to the hostel to pick them up, they kept asking where we'd been for the past two days. Another thing we couldn't hide was the smell; you can't put that amount of hash and opium in a confined space without its pungent aroma pervading the whole of it. So we did tell them, because it was quite obvious, and to placate them, we promised them free drugs until they were dropped off in India, which they were all more than happy with. They also liked the idea of being involved, as they now became drug smugglers too, which added a whole new dimension to their adventure. Our next stop was at a market to buy enough incense to burn to help cover the smell. Then we headed for the next border, which was another famous landmark.

13

The Khyber Pass was somewhere we'd all heard of, although only Gary and John had been here before. It was the main place in the north to cross between Afghanistan and Pakistan, which meant heading back into those Hindu Kush mountains, only this time to the east towards Islamabad. The pass itself had a long history of lawlessness, where tribesmen would wait on the cliffs on either side of the road and take potshots at the passing vehicles. It was also known for its firearms market, where you could buy replicas of many types of guns and rifles (although you took your life in your hands if you tried to fire them, because they were made from inferior quality metals and could explode in your face at any time).

When we did get to the border on the Afghan side, there was a certain amount of nervousness in the coach because of the drugs we were transporting. Even after burning a lot of incense to cover the smell, there was still an uneasiness, but it was all unnecessary, as we sailed through customs with just the aid of a bottle of scotch. However, we still had to wait in a compound for more vehicles to arrive, as the customs guards would only send convoys of four or more vehicles through at a time, in case of breakdowns. This was so one of the other vehicles could give you a tow if you did have a problem, as again there wasn't exactly an AA man to phone for help. And you were then at the mercy of the tribesmen waiting on the cliffs.

This gave us time to check the coach over before we did leave. I wasn't quite sure what to expect when we did head through. I was thinking of it only being a few miles, but it turned out to be thirty-three miles (fifty-five kilometres) of winding road through craggy ravines; at times, the road wasn't much wider than the coach. I listened for shots fired by the tribesmen, who I could see sitting on horses up on the cliffs, but didn't hear any. It looked like they were just watching and waiting for somebody to break down, then they would attack, but thankfully, that didn't happen. All the vehicles got through with no mechanical mishaps.

Pakistan customs caused us a bit of a problem when we did get through the pass, because at first, the guards wanted all the passengers off with their passports. That is, until John did his thing with a bottle of scotch, but it also took a carton of cigarettes to placate these guards.

So now, as we headed off into Pakistan, there was another choice to make: either stay on the main road going east towards Islamabad and Lahore, then on to Delhi in India, or turn right at Peshawar, which would take us south along the Indus River towards Hyderabad and Karachi. This was, as Gary pointed out, the slower route, but it was more direct because our priority now was to get the load we were transporting to Ahmadabad ASAP.

So the decision was made for us, as we headed south to witness the beautiful sight of lush greens, deep blues, and mahogany browns as the Indus River delta opened up before us. It was good to see something different, other than range after range of mountains that seemed to make up northern Pakistan and Afghanistan, although we still had the Sulaiman Mountain range to our right as we travelled down this road. This whole area was the industry and breadbasket of the surrounding countries, all thanks to that mighty Indus River. Its source lay somewhere high up in the mountains where Tibet lay, in the Himalayas.

Our progress was slowed even more by the first puncture of our trip, which didn't come as a surprise because this road was often little more than a dirt track. However, it did give everybody a chance to get off the coach to stretch their legs while the wheel was changed. After it was, we were off again, now heading for Mithankot, where we crossed the Indus River. Then we headed away from the river delta towards Islamgarh and the Cholistan Desert, with India waiting on the other side of it.

"Burn lots of incense," Gary kept saying as we got closer to the border, "because the Indian border guards are always suspicious of coaches like this."

He'd crossed here before and knew the Pakistanis would just wave us through, which they did. This seemed to be the pattern with most countries along the way: no problem leaving, but a search when you entered. I just hoped this wasn't going to turn into another Switzerland, because again it was a small border crossing, only the circumstances were very different this time. However, there was more trouble to come on this journey from crossing borders, only it would be Steve's turn to fall foul of some Indian border guards. But that was later.

Now, though, Gary was looking for a guard he knew, who he could easily bribe, but he wasn't sure if the guard was working that day. Otherwise, it meant taking a chance, which is what we had to do, anyway, because there was no sign of Gary's guard when we were flagged down at the barrier.

Then, and you could clearly see the relief on Gary's face, the guard he wanted appeared from inside the customs post. There was a smile as they greeted each other, a shake of hands, then an exchange of goods (scotch and cigarettes this time). The gate was then lifted, and we were through; once we were clear of the border post, a mighty cheer of relief went up from everybody on board.

It was only after we were through that Gary told us, "If we had been caught with that amount of drugs, it would have probably meant twenty years in an Indian prison for all of us."

He thought it best not tell us before, so as not to heighten our already nervous state.

14

The Promised Land, that's what it felt like I'd reached, once we crossed the India border, which had been like an impossible dream when I was locked up in Switzerland only a few weeks ago. Now I was actually here. I had this picture in my head of it all being jungles and forests, but instead, we were in the middle of the Thar Desert, with the only sign of life being the border we'd just crossed. If we'd hadn't turned right at Peshawar to head south and carry on going east toward Delhi, then we would have come to the jungles and forests.

It wouldn't be until we got into the Gujarat Province, closer to Ahmadabad, that some greenery would return. So now with no more borders to cross, apart from internal ones, there was a much more relaxed feel to the journey. Everybody onboard had been together for nearly two weeks now, so there was a real bond starting to develop between us all. Even Liza and Lucy had become more involved, rather than keeping to themselves, like they did at the start of the journey. The Thar Desert, which seemed to go on forever, made up most of the state of Rajasthan, where we'd entered India. The first major town we came to was Jaisalmer; it was like being dropped into classic twelfth-century India and came as a welcomed break from that endless hot desert. We managed to talk Gary into staying for a few hours, so we could have a look around the place.

Built mainly in and around the Jaisalmer fort, which was famous in the area for being the site of many historic battles, the town was full of temples containing that instantly recognisable intricate Indian architecture. Carving those multilimbed gods, goddesses, and animals must have taken such patience. The whole town was dominated by the Maharaja Palace, which had beautiful panoramic views from its towers. It was the perfect way to watch the sun set before we headed back onto that desert plain for the cooler night drive towards Radhanpur, the next stop on our journey.

15

Distance was another thing on this journey, as I myself had only driven from northern Europe to Greece a couple of times and that being mainly on decent roads. The distances we were covering now were vast in comparison, and on roads that were little more than dirt tracks at times. However, with John, Steve, Don, and me sharing the driving, there was never a problem with driver fatigue, which made a big difference. According to John, who'd done this return trip nine times before, the journey was normally made with two drivers, which was much more tiring and therefore more dangerous, mainly because of boulders and potholes in the road. They were more of a problem at night because of the reduced visibility, and there weren't exactly any street lights on these desolate roads to help see what was coming and guide your way.

This did slow our progress to some extent, but with four of us, we could split into twos and have one person driving while another watched in for anything in the road. Don and I were the less experienced, so we usually took the easier day shift, leaving John and Steve on nights. Once Don and I got some experience, the shifts evened out. It was good to have that extra pair of eyes watching those unpredictable roads, and it did save us a number of times hitting both boulders and potholes.

So we could just keep rolling until we needed more diesel, as long as nothing went wrong with the coach, that is. Up until that point, apart from the airbag that needed to be replaced in Iran and the puncture in Pakistan, it had performed perfectly.

This is where I have to mention John again, because having him along for the journey was a real asset. Not only for his border skills, which had been a great help smoothing our way from country to country, but also for his intimate knowledge of the coach we were travelling in. He knew just what maintenance needed to be done along the way, and if there was a problem, he knew just how to fix it. I never really got to know him that well in the Dam; he'd been away driving with Steve most of the time, plus I was locked up in Switzerland. It was only now on this epic journey that I got the chance to find out more about him.

Originally from Bedford in the UK and in his early thirties, he had gotten the wanderlust in his early twenties, so went travelling to France, Spain, and Holland. That was where he'd met the Magic Bus guys and found what was the perfect job for him: being able to earn money and travel at the same time, only not in a conventional way, which is what the Magic Bus service was all about. This I will say again was perfect for him, and he'd been driving for them for almost ten years now. This was the experience he was bringing with him and we were able to draw on, and it was very much appreciated by everybody on board. And all that time on the road had filled him with amazing stories, which he took great pleasure in regaling to anyone who would listen.

He also turned out to be a demon backgammon player, which I'll tell you about next.

16

Backgammon was something Don taught me to play on the boat back in the Dam; it helped while away many hours crossing those endless dusty plains or traversing serpentine mountain roads. So we have to thank Don for bringing his backgammon board along, because whenever we weren't driving, sleeping, or staring out the window watching the world go by, we'd be gammoning away. It was like still having a little bit of the Dam and boat with us, which was appreciated by nearly all the passengers on board, because after a few days, most of them wanted to play too. So to give a chance to all those who did want to play, an intercoach competition was organised. This also added more interest to the games, rather than just playing for fun.

By the time we got as far as India, all the participants had played each other at least once over a three-leg game, and all the winners from those games went into the next round. There'd also been time for rivalries to develop between the winning players, with everybody else on board betting money or drugs on the games, which added even more spice to it all.

For the final rounds, a playing area was set up on the back seat, normally set aside for the sleeping driver. And to add extra atmosphere, the games would take place at night, when there was no daylight to distract from the play. Then to add even more interest, the games were extended to the best of seven. So on game nights, the coach would be buzzing with people playing, or waiting to play, or watching the game.

I'd like to say here that I went on to win the competition, but that wouldn't be true. I lost in the third round to John, who went on to win the whole thing. He beat Hans, one of the German passengers, in the final. Don also did better than me, getting into the semi-finals, where he lost to Hans. The competition was a great success; it not only helped to bring everybody on board even closer but also added interest to those long night drives, when it was difficult to sleep in the confines of the coach, and you couldn't see out the window. The only disappointment was we didn't have time to do it all again, as everybody enjoyed it so much. Now, though, we were getting close to Ahmadabad, where most of the passengers were getting off.

17

"Enlightenment" is a word I used earlier; I remember Gary using it to describe his first trip to the East, during one of our many conversations back on the boat. How right he was, because I thought my first journey through northern Europe to Greece had opened my eyes, but it really was a different world once you got into Turkey, with Iran, Afghanistan, and Pakistan, all of which I wished I had more time to explore rather than just watch out the coach window.

However, now we had reached India, it was like a full metal (or mental) jacket assault on my senses, as this amazing place picked me up and spun my world around again. And the colours; well, it looked like a bomb had gone off in a paint factory, with bright vivid shades of the rainbow everywhere. This still influences my life today, I think, because I still love to use bright primary colours in my artwork.

Now with most of the journey already done, there was more time to explore the places we were passing through, although Gary did keep reminding us that the sooner we got to Ahmadabad and unloaded our cargo, the sooner we could really relax and enjoy the trip. Even though it wouldn't actually be until we got to Goa, before all the drugs were finally unloaded.

Radhanpur, our second stop in India, was like Jaisalmer: another beautiful old walled city, which marked the end of the Thar Desert, finally bringing us back to something more than just hot dusty plains. Now there was actually some green vegetation. Radhanpur was smaller than Jaisalmer but just as aged, with lots more of that amazing, intricate architecture. We didn't stay too long, just drove around its centre and then on to a garage to top up with diesel on the way out of town. That would be enough to get us to Ahmadabad.

Going from Jaisalmer to Radhanpur, we had to cross our first internal border going from Rajasthan to Gujarat, which did have a lot of security, but again, Gary used his magic to ease our way through. After that, he seemed to relax a bit, and the closer we got to our next stop, Ahmadabad, told us what we should expect when we got there.

His contact's name was Raj, who was quite a character. He was a lawyer by profession, but I don't think it was like any lawyer you'd find in the West (although not knowing any lawyers myself at the time, maybe he was). Anyway, Raj had his fingers in many pies, anything that would make him money, it seemed: hotels, boarding houses, rented apartments, cafes. He also had an interest in a couple of brothels, which did come as a surprise to me, thinking they only existed in the decadent West, not somewhere like religious India, with all its religious statues and temples. That's when I realised that sex was a big seller all over the world and of course they did come up with the ultimate guide to sex, the Karman Sutra.

Last but not least came the drugs; Raj was also connected to a number of opium dens in the city, so he'd be very interested in the Afghani opium we were transporting. Its quality was always in demand and fetched a premium price when sold, making it very good for all concerned.

From a distance, Ahmadabad came as quite a surprise, because it looked like a fairly modern Western city, with the first high-rise building I'd seen since Tehran. However, when we did get into the suburbs, it was the poverty that came as a shock. This blew away the whole concept of thinking I'd grown up in poverty myself; what I was looking at made my experience look like I'd had everything: a roof over my head, clothes on my back, and food in my stomach.

Here, the kids who quickly surrounded the coach whenever we stopped had little more than rags for clothes, which in this scorching heat wasn't that important, I guess. What humbled me the most: There wasn't a glum face amongst them, just all smiles as they begged, looking up at the windows of the coach for anything we'd give them. I guess that's the innocence of childhood, only being aware of what's around you and not the wider world that exists outside: a bit like the way I'd grown up.

Both John and Gary told us not to interact with them because if we did give the kids something, we'd never get rid of them, but it was hard not to when you saw the poverty they lived in. Gary then talked about the Indian caste system and started to go into the whole psychology behind Indian family life, how the lower caste parents would have a lot of children so there'd be more of them to beg.

However, that's a whole different book in itself, so we won't go there.

18

Sleep properly: that's what I was really looking forward to the most, because after nearly two weeks on the road, and catching only a couple of nights not having to sleep on the coach, what a welcome sight it was, the prospects of a few days in Ahmadabad, with a proper shower and a comfortable bed to sleep in.

We arrived in the centre of the city, which was like another planet compared to the suburbs (or should I say slums) surrounding it. Raj's offices and main hotel weren't a disappointment. This was one of the best hotels in the city; it was called Raj's Palace, which summed up the man himself, as he was no disappointment, either, being larger than life in every sense of the word, and like most wealthy Indian people, pale and well rounded (or should I say fat).

Welcoming us with open arms and big smiles, he got straight onto organising rooms for everybody who was staying. Then after we were all settled and showered, there was food and drink in the beautifully ornate dining room, decorated in a classic Indian way. This meal turned into an impromptu party, because as I said before, most of our passengers were leaving us now. We headed off to Porbandar (Mahatma Gandhi's birthplace), a short train ride away on the Kathiawar Peninsula, but as we were to find out for ourselves later on this journey, even a short train ride in this country could take hours (or even days), as it wasn't exactly British Rail.

A celebration was just what we needed after being on the move for so long. Even Gary could relax now, that is, after the drugs were unloaded from the coach and put in Raj's office safe until we made the deal. So the party began and went on well into the night; the noise we were making also attracted some of the other hotel guests, but everybody was welcome.

This was when, after a number of failed attempts to get into Liza and Lucy's pants, my luck suddenly changed; they spent the whole night chatting me up, and then I found myself about one in the morning in their hotel room, having very drunken sex with both of them. I only wish I'd not been so drunk so I could remember more, but sadly, that night's activities are just a blur.

However, I do remember being woken up the following day by the pair of them, taking it in turns to suck on my morning chubby. This is one of the best ways to wake up, and that memory will always stay with me. I then returned the favour, by going down on them, and after that, we then spent the next hour f**king each other's brains outs. So the night of rest I was looking forward to turned into something much better: another amazing sexual adventure (or what I can remember of it, only not on the scale of the one in Belgium after I was released from prison, but that would take some beating).

"So why me and why now?" I asked, as we laid back in the afterglow of that morning's sexual activities.

"Well," Liza replied, "you were so good to us after the attempted rape in Iran; we wanted to pay you back in some way."

"And this will be our last chance," Lucy added, "as we're now leaving to head to the coast."

"Well, I can't let you go without one more for the road now, can I?" I said, before I when muff-diving again, leaving them to canoodle with each other. I was soon hard again and finished them off in style, by f**king their brains out one last time.

When the three of us entered the hotel lobby together, all smiling and laughing, Steve looked like he couldn't believe it at first; that is, until they both kissed me. He then had this big grin as he came over, trying to be subtle by winking at me, which gave the whole game away, and we all started laughing again. Anyway, it was enough to make him realise I had done what most of the other men on the coach wanted to do: shag both Liza and Lucy.

It's funny how the previous night's antics almost felt like a dream, because when we went outside to where Don and the rest of the passenger were, I was hit again by the full experience of a bustling Indian city at eleven in the morning. This was something that took getting used to; Western cities seemed so sedate in comparison. However, here we were all together on the coach for the last time, heading to the train station to drop off the departing passengers.

There were lots of bleary eyes and weary faces from the previous night's partying, as we all said our farewells, overshadowed by a sense of sadness that this was our last time together. The journey we'd just experienced together had been such an enlightening one. Even though most of us were strangers at the start, in a relatively short time, we cemented a real bond. So as we were about to go our separate ways, there were some tears as we did part.

19

The deal with Raj came next. He was waiting for us at the hotel when we returned from the station. So Gary, John, Don, Steve, and I headed for his office, and the process began. First, Raj wanted to test the product, so he brought in Ramesh, who worked at one of Raj's opium dens as his official tester. Ramesh, from the look of him, had spent too much time indoors, because for an Indian, he was almost as pale as me, which was probably down to him working in said opium den, where days could go by without any exposure to the outside world.

Ramesh had turned into what looked like a white man. He was also quite small compared to Raj, which wasn't difficult, I guess, as Raj was quite large, as I said before. It was hard to judge Ramesh's age; his size and complexion did give him a youthful look, but on closer inspection, there were lines around his eyes. So at a guess, I would have said he was probably in his early forties, like Raj.

So the testing began, with a plaque of hash and opium being taken from the safe. The age old process involved breaking open the plaque of hash, with a burst of fresh hashish aroma filling the office. Then Ramesh inspected it, checking the colour, which was a lovely deep green and brown. This seemed to satisfied him, as he gave us a nod of approval. He then broke off a small piece and heated it with some matches he took from his pocket. The hashish aroma was amplified even more as the hash started to burn, filling the air with smoke, which he then inhaled.

In fact, we all inhaled the smoke, so much of it filled the room. It was a deep, satisfying aroma, that delivered an almost-instant high. This is when we were all happy we'd paid the extra money and bought the best-quality hash, because there was no way to fault the stuff.

Ramesh then went through the same process with the opium, only this time, he didn't burn it as much, just enough to get a flavour but not too much to knock him out. We then got that same nod of approval, so that concluded the testing; next came the bartering.

This started with Raj and Ramesh going into a huddle and talking in their local dialect, which sounded a bit like a strange kind of Welsh, almost making me think I was in the valleys back in the UK for a moment. However, their talk didn't take long before Raj said in English he wanted to buy the whole shipment. This wasn't possible; Gary planned to only sell half now and take the rest on to Goa, where he knew people were waiting for it and we could make more money by selling it in smaller quantities.

So now the price and quantities went back and forth, until a decision was made: three-quarters of the opium and half of the hash at a price, according to Gary, well over the normal asking rate.

Now that was settled to everyone's satisfaction, and with most of our passengers off on their own journeys, we could relax and spend a few more days checking out Ahmadabad before heading on to Goa, our final destination, or so I thought. What I hadn't taken into consideration was Steve feeling bored and then getting himself arrested over a simple thing like a nut that we all enjoy.

20

Pistachio nuts are cheap and readily available in India; however, to a businessman like Raj, who brought them by the 500-kilo sack to supply his hotels and café, they still cost too much. So he would send a truck just over the border into Pakistan once a month to buy them there, because he could make a significant saving this way.

The problem was, the truck he normally used was unavailable, so a plan was hatched between Raj and Steve to do the journey using the coach. Under normal circumstances, this would have been fine and added a little more profit to all concerned. Only normal circumstances weren't at play here, and this journey would lead to the second term of incarceration during this adventure, only it would be Steve's turn this time.

Now the truth of what really happened will probably never be known, due to Steve's embarrassment over this whole affair; I never did find out all the details. However, I'll tell you the story from what I heard, which started with him going to a small market town called Umarkot, just over the Pakistan border.

Steve left early on the fourth day, with Ahmed, Raj's usual driver, showing him the way, leaving the rest of us still enjoying Raj's hospitality; in fact, we were all lost in one of his opium dens.

John did offer to go along, but Steve, in his usual self-assured way, said, "It's okay; I can handle it myself."

Well, not taking John was his first mistake; I'm sure he would have been a great help at the border, because Ahmed showed up that evening without Steve or the bus, telling us our friend had been arrested for trying to smuggle pistachio nuts into the country.

Anyway, from what I could understand from Ahmed's broken English, Steve had somehow upset the border guards when he tried to bribe them. He'd laid the sacks of nuts down the centre aisle of the coach, making no attempt to cover them. Then, he offered a mere ten dollars as a bribe, instead of what should have been fifty. So the coach and nuts had been impounded, with Steve being locked up in the local jail.

Now that certainly brought us back to earth with a very large bump, and there we were, all floating in an opiate haze, where we'd been lost for the past two days in Raj's best opium den, a dark cool place where your every whim was catered to by people like Ramesh, while you lay on soft warm carpets with a pillow to support your head, being fed opium pipes whenever you wanted them. It almost felt like being back your mother's womb, only I can't remember being there, but if I did, I'm sure it would have felt like this. Floating in that warm amniotic fluid, being fed your food through the umbilical cord whenever you needed it; sounds familiar, doesn't it?

Anyway, now I was reborn again out of that opium den womb and my opiate haze to help get Steve out of jail and also watch Raj swing into action and be what he was supposed to be: a lawyer.

21

Easy; I'd like to say it was easy to get Steve out of jail, but even with Raj being a lawyer, we still went through all the procedures and departments. As you can imagine, Indian bureaucracy turned it into a nightmare of paperwork and bribery, which went all the way to the top, and the higher you got, the bigger the bribes became. We were well past a bottle of scotch or a carton of cigarettes to ease the way. Now it was cold hard cash, and only American dollars spoke the right words; none of the local rupees were acceptable here.

The problem turned out to be the person Steve upset at the border wasn't just a guard; he was the captain of the customs post, who was now doing everything in his power to keep Steve locked up until he had milked every last bit of whatever he could get from the situation. What he saw, I'm sure, was a Western cash cow with a full udder, and he was going to suckle on the teat until it was completely dry. So now this simple journey for nuts, which was supposed to earn us money, had turned into a fight for Steve's life.

This was where Raj's help became essential, because he knew the system and how to manipulate it. So the bartering began, and not to relegate Steve's position, but a certain amount was first negotiated to get the coach back and then the same for the nuts, leaving Steve to last, who by that stage had been moved from the local jail to a much larger prison closer to Ahmadabad, where we could visit him. When we did, it made my stay in a Swiss jail look like a holiday camp, because this place was like hell on earth, with overcrowded cells and rundown, crumbling buildings. This, combined with the open sewers running through the place, and the body odour of so many unwashed inmates, made it smell like an overripe fish market that been in the sun too long; I felt nauseous from the moment I entered.

Under the circumstances, Steve looked quite calm when we first saw him, but after he described the conditions of his cell, I think he started to realise just how bad it was, because by the time we left, he was on his knees, begging us to get him out of there ASAP.

As we told him, that was down to the captain, who was making it very difficult, even after being paid the money he asked for. Whatever Steve had said to him at the border had left a real mark, so even Raj was at a loss of what to do next. At our next meeting with the captain, he managed to get Steve moved to a different cell, which was a lot better than the first one, because it was at the side of the prison, where the cells opened up to a courtyard. During the day, the prisoners could be outside and not stuck inside with that nauseating stench. And the food; well, the only thing that saved him from having to eat the roach-infested rice that the other inmates ate were our regular visits from the outside; we brought him fresh food, water, and drugs to keep him healthy and sane while he was there. In fact, we all spent many an afternoon getting stoned and playing chequers or backgammon with him until he was released.

That took almost four weeks, and the thing that finally brokered the deal was my Seiko watch, which was the last thing I had to connect me to the Western world. The captain demanded it as a final payment, and I was more than happy to part with it to get Steve out of that hellhole.

Steve always wanted a nickname, so now it was my turn to christen him with one, which was "Nut." Only because of the circumstances it came under, he never did like it, so I won't use it.

22

Cost: Well, those pistachio nuts must have been the most expensive in the world by the time Raj did get them. Cashwise, it must have been around two thousand dollars to pay all the bribes to get everything back. Then on top of that was my Seiko watch, which was worth around $350. There was also the time it took, but nobody was going anywhere until we got everything back, because we didn't have the coach (and Steve, of course). The few passengers who did want to go on to Goa were either happy to wait with us or accepted train tickets and went on their way.

However, on the morning of the twenty-seventh day, we were all at the prison to see Steve set free. I can't tell you how relieved we all were to see him walk out of that place, because even with Raj's help, there were still times when we couldn't be sure just how long it would take. Even though we'd all spent time with him in there, that still didn't stop us from hugging him, as we whooped and hollered at his release.

We then spent the next two days making up for lost time, partying first at Raj's hotel and then moving on to one of his brothels, which I have to say was a lot better than I imagined. The image I had in my head was of a seedy, rundown building, full of equally unattractive whores. Only that wasn't the case; in fact, the place was like a temple filled with vestal virgins (well, maybe not virgins, as the women were there to have sex, but the quality of them was a very pleasant surprise). We had an orgy that lasted two days, I think. It was reminiscent of the parties we had at the Inside Out Club back in the Dam and the bordello in Belgium, after I got out of jail in Switzerland. Only this time, I had to share the girls. It now seemed to me that like opium dens, brothels were much alike, wherever you went in the world.

There was a plan to spend a third day at one of Raj's opium dens, which would have probably turned into more once we were there, only by then, Gary wanted to get back on the road, as his people in Goa were waiting for the hash and opium. So we reluctantly brought the party to an end and gathered our things and then loaded the drugs back onto the coach before setting off again. Because of our extended stay at Raj's hotel due to Steve's incarceration, we'd become very friendly with all the staff, so it was a bit like when we'd left the Dam, with everybody on the street shaking our hands and waving goodbye. All that was missing was the ticker tape and banners wishing us a good trip.

23

Bombay would be our next stop, where three of our last six passengers were getting off. That was still a three-day drive, going through Vadodara and Surat, heading south down the west coast of the country, with the Gulf of Khambha to our right. It did feel good to be back on the road again after our unexpected prolonged stay in Ahmadabad. But now that we'd lost most of our passengers, there wasn't the same atmosphere on the coach like before.

That's one of the things I really enjoyed before we got to Ahmadabad; over the time we'd been on this journey, almost forty strangers had become a close-knit tribe of travellers, all looking out for each other, like when Liza and Lucy were attacked in Iran, and everybody rallied around to help them. Even when we had the backgammon competition, there'd been no animosity between players, just a good sense of rivalry to add some spice to the games.

I now started to understand why John found this way of life so addictive; it was like a drug, this pull of the open road and the constantly changing panorama going past the window. It became almost hypnotic. That's where the real hook was, I think, because you had this constant need to keep pushing on, hoping that everything would hold together until your next stop and then your final destination. Even if you were travelling the same roads in such desolate extreme places, you never knew what new adventure could be waiting for you around the next corner, which made the odds of something happening to you a lot shorter.

The other thing for me when we'd started out on this journey was actually getting to our destination. When you considered the distance we were about to travel, it looked almost impossible. It was like a mirage that was always just out of reach. Only now, as we headed out of Ahmadabad and were well into India, the thought of actually getting to Goa did start to settle in my head.

Gary had talked a lot about the place when we were in the Dam, which had fired my imagination, making my desire to see the place even stronger. Only now, I was in touching distance of finding out if reality lived up to my imagination, which under most other circumstances was never the case.

24

First, however, we had the small matter of negotiating our next internal border, going from Gujarat, just passing Dadra and Nagar Haveli on our left, and into the state of Maharashtra. Because of Gary's consummate border skills, this went without a hitch. So we were now heading for our next stop, Bombay, and if I thought Ahmadabad was an experience, then I certainly wasn't ready for the *Dr Strangelove* nuclear explosion of Bombay, because it surpassed Ahmadabad in every way, from the abject poverty that surrounded the city, to the unbounded wealth at the centre of it.

Bombay was known as the gateway to India, being at the mouth of the Ulhas River. From all the trade that passed through it over its many centuries of existence, it had become the most densely populated city in India, with about 7 million people at the time. That became very clear as we tried to make our way to the main train station but spent most of the time stuck in another traffic jam, only this one must have been the biggest in the world (well, the biggest one I'd ever seen, anyway).

We were heading for one of the biggest transport hubs in the world because Gary had the idea to make some extra cash by touting for more passengers wanting to go south to Goa. We were down to only three, so this was a good idea. So while he, Don, and Steve stayed with the coach to round up possible new passengers, John and I went off to find fresh supplies of food and water. This led us to a local market behind the station, where we witnessed just how efficient the Indian people were at using every scrap of food available to them. As we entered the market, there was a dead donkey on the ground in front of a stall. From the look of it, it had certainly lived a full life, and that's being kind to this poor creature, as it lay crumpled in a heap.

About an hour later (although it was hard tell now, as I didn't have my watch), we were coming back past the stall, only to find the donkey had been hung, drawn, and quartered, then laid out on the stall with its head ceremonially placed at the centre of the display. As I said before, I don't think it was doing it any favours, from the look of the poor animal. Only now to add to the whole presentation, it was covered in flies too.

I was very glad I wasn't consuming any of that meat, and just seeing what had happened would have been enough to turn most hardened meat-eaters into vegetarians, which I myself had become anyway, on the advice of both Gary and John. Once you got into Turkey and even before that in Greece, you had to be very careful of eating the meat, as our soft Western systems weren't hardened enough to handle most of the fresh food that was available in these Eastern countries. Even the fruit and vegetables could give you a good case of Delhi belly, as it was known locally, or the shits, if you want its Western name.

The problem lay with the water, which was used to grow the produce. You could never be sure of its condition, so even if you used bottled water to clean the fruit and veg before you ate it, it could be contaminated from the water used when it was grown, which made eating any fresh produce a bit like Russian roulette. So the key to eating was, try to find canned goods, as the food was processed so wasn't contaminated in any way, and of course, always drink bottled water, which now, as we were heading back to the coach, we'd managed to secure both of from a small supermarket on the far side of the market.

25

Full, the bus was as we headed out of Bombay, going as fast as the constant traffic jam would allow us. Gary looking very pleased with himself, as his plan had worked, because in a little over two hours, thirty more passengers had been rounded up, which had netted another three hundred dollars to go into the pot. This would be more than enough to cover all the coach's expenses for the trip so far. And if nothing else went wrong, it would cover our food and water too. Steve was especially appreciative of this, because he was playing catch-up now, after losing a thousand dollars getting the coach and pistachio nuts back plus getting himself out of prison back in Ahmadabad, with the other thousand dollars being paid by his co-conspirator Raj.

Anyway, now with a full coach again and smiles on all our faces, we were heading for our final destination: Goa, one of the smallest states in India. To be more specific, we went first to Panaji, the state's capital, to drop off the passengers and sell some of the drugs we had left. Then on to Butterfly Beach, which was close to the town of Palolem, where our journey would end (for the moment, anyway). Only first there was the small matter of the three-day drive to get to Panaji, which would take us down a part of the coastline where the earliest signs of human life in India were found. Then of course came our last internal border, going from Maharashtra into Goa at Pernem. Because of a dispute between the two states, it turned out to be the trickiest we'd encountered so far, but after a certain amount of bribery and Gary's magic words, we got through without a search. These disputes between states seemed to be the norm, because it was the same in the north, where there was a long history of fighting, which did contradict India being a place of peace and tranquillity, as there seemed to be problems between a lot of states there.

The thing that had changed was the terrain, which had gone from the dry barren deserts of Gujarat state in the north of the country to lush, verdant greens of tropical forests and jungles as we got closer to Goa. The temperature hadn't changed much; it had been hot ever since we'd entered the country. It was the humidity that had changed, from a dry heat in the north, which was much easier to deal with, to now feeling like you were taking a shower every time you left the confines of our lovely air-conditioned coach, because you became instantly covered in sweat. This took some getting used to for a cold-blooded northern European boy like myself, but after a few days, it just became a part of everyday life and was a small price to pay for the tropical beauty that surrounded us.

Gary was so right about this place, though, because it was something special and did cast a spell over you. Well, it did over him, as he'd been back here every winter for almost ten years now. However, for me, it wouldn't be until we reached Butterfly Beach when I would understand the real beauty of this place, with my imagination and reality finally becoming one.

26

Wonder, I did back in June, what India would look like, when I stood up at the Acropolis looking out over ancient Athens during my first journey on this adventure. Now after we'd travelled about halfway down the country, I realised just what a diverse place India was. From the walled cities of Jaisalmer and Judhpur in the north, through Ahmadabad and Bombay, with their extreme poverty and wealth, to now as we approached Panaji, the capital city of Goa, that from a distance looked to have more of a Mediterranean feel. That was probably down to the Portuguese, who conquered this part of India in the sixteenth century and stayed for 450 years.

Only to call Panaji a city was really doing it a favour, because if it had been in England, it would have been called a large town at best. However, it was a very picturesque place as we drove into the centre, with its brightly painted terraced buildings going down to the sea, some with colourful roof tiles that really set the place alight. More of that Indian colour, which was so part of the country's magic. This is where we would drop off our last passengers, after we'd released the rest at Karmali train station on the way into the city, and before we headed further south. Only now with our last three passengers leaving us, who'd been with us since the Dam, it really was the end of the main part of our journey. However, there was still time for one last party, so we celebrated in style, because they'd really had become part of our crew in the time we'd all been together.

Gary was now directing John, who was driving to what looked like a café near the beach to the north of the city. The ground level part of the place did sell food and drinks. Only that was just a front for what was really going there, because we were then taken down some dark, mysterious stairs at the back of the place, to find the real purpose of what was going on there. It involved taking drugs, and you guessed it: It was another opium den.

Only here, because this part of Panaji was very touristy, you weren't limited to just opium. In fact, it was like being back in the Dam, because it was a drug-taker's heaven, as there were various types of hash for sale. From the local Indian charras to Nepalese temple balls, Kashmir twist and sticks, Afghani black, and red and gold Lebanese. There were three types of heroin from China, Pakistan, and Malaysia, and if that wasn't enough, Colombian cocaine was also available.

We were then ushered into a back room to meet Pan, the owner, who was interested in buying some of our hash and opium. So a deal was struck to sell half of both the hash and opium to him, before we were then given the full VIP treatment, which included servants at our beck and call. So for the next three days, it was like we'd died and gone to drug nirvana, as we were served at some point with everything that was available there. I say three days, but I really can't be sure just how long we were lost in that place, not that it mattered, anyway, because our job was done. Now our time was our own to do what we liked.

There was one other thing available, which I neglected to mention before; that was sex. We spent the last day there in a bathhouse on the floor below the opium den, having our every sexual desire satisfied by some very attractive young ladies. Wow, what a place. I never even found out the name of it, but if it was going to be called anything, it had to be Pan's Paradise.

Gary had now officially become a legend in all our eyes, after everything he'd done on the journey so far, and there was still one more thing to come. Only that waited for us when we got to Palolem.

27

Miss: You could easily overlook the road to Palolem from the main highway, because there was a signpost, but it was like the road: very small. The road itself looked more like a track that wouldn't lead anywhere. However, we couldn't have gone more than a hundred yards down it before it was like we'd entered another world, as the forest/jungle of tall palm trees enveloped us. As we went farther, it got so dense in places, John, who was driving, had to put the coach's headlights on to see the way. Only now, as we did go deeper into this strange new world, what really became freaky were the noises, what I can only describe as these strange high-pitched shrieks, that at first scared the shit out of us. Gary assured us it was only the birds calling and that all the large predators had been wiped out in this part of India. What you did have to look out for, though, were the snakes and spiders, because some of them could be dangerous. And if you did get bitten, the nearest medical facility was back in Panaji.

We followed the road for what must have been two miles, going as fast as it would let us, before the trees started to thin out, and this beautiful bay started to appear through them. Then further ahead, a collection of what I can only describe as wooden shacks started to appear, which I assumed was Palolem itself. Then as the trees ended at the beach, we could see about twenty small boats on the shoreline, surrounded by what turned out to be the local fishermen. They'd just returned from their day's fishing and were sorting out the catch, only on hearing the coach, they all came running to welcome us.

This is again where Gary came into his own, because it was like a long-lost hero had returned, as they shouted his name and surrounded him, shaking his hand and patting him on the back. All the noise and commotion brought our arrival to the attention of the rest of the people, who appeared from the direction of the wooden shacks. That's when the party really started, as Gary was ushered to the local bar, and the drinking began. Some of the fishermen did go back to their boats to finish sorting out their catch, but they soon returned to what had turned into quite a party, which I soon realised was for the benefit of us all, as we were welcomed by everyone there.

Another thing I started to notice amongst all the smiling Indian faces were some distinctly Western features, which turned out to be a collection of hippies or dropouts; I wasn't quite sure what to call them. Like Gary, they had found this place, fallen in love with it, and returned whenever they could. Some of them never left; why would they, the lucky bastards? The party went on well into the night, as we were introduced to this local hooch, which was distilled from coconut milk and had a real kick to it. In fact, it was so good and so freely handed out, I can't remember much about what did happen that night. Just waking up the following morning, face down in the sand, with a thick head. It must have taken me a good half an hour before my head and eyes started to clear, and I realised I'd woken up in paradise.

The view up the beach that appeared in front of my eyes was of perfect silvery sand and tall, sweeping palm trees that reached up to an azure sky, which was all set off by the pale blue waters of the Arabian Sea lapping the shore. It was like something I'd only ever seen on a picture postcard before. This is where my imagination and reality did finally meet, because the image I had in my head was more than matched by the view I was looking at here.

28

*"**Six months** since I've seen that view, and every time I get back to see it again, I realise it's worth the effort."*

It was Gary's voice that broke the spell the view had put me under, as he sat down beside me. And he was so right, as we sat in the early morning sunshine, soaking it all in, me with the extra pleasure of seeing such a beautiful sight for the first time. We were then joined by Don, John, and Steve, who were just as transfixed by the beautiful vista stretching out before us. We all thanked Gary again for bringing us to this magical place.

After being on the road for almost two months (which admittedly did include an enforced three-and-a-half-week stay in Ahmadabad while Steve was in prison), now all we wanted to do was sit back, relax, and do nothing for a while, with Palolem being the perfect place to do just that.

In fact, according to John, there was nothing to do now until the beginning of May next year, when the Magic Bus trail opened again. That gave us almost six months to just laze around in paradise. However, before the lazing could begin, there were some loose ends to tidy up. Only first, I couldn't resist the pull of the Arabian Sea, and my first swim in it, which at that time of the morning was still cool and refreshing and helped clear my head. Then after a good hour of happily splashing around, it was back to the coach to dry off and to tie up those loose ends that needed tying.

Now I had a chance to see Palolem properly for the first time, which looked so perfectly in tune with its surroundings. Nestled where the road in and out ended, and where beach and forest/jungle met, it really did complete the picture-perfect paradise Gary had implanted in my head back in the Dam. Only calling it a town was like calling Panaji a city: doing it a big favour, as the place was little more than a village by Western standards. However, it certainly didn't look like any Western village I'd ever seen before, with the buildings raised three feet off the ground, in case of flooding during the monsoon rains, and being mainly built out of wood and palm tree leaves. I guess that made sense, as we were surrounded by the stuff, so you didn't have to go too far to get it.

Another noticeable thing here was the absence of poverty, so prevalent in the big cities. No sign of children running around begging. In fact, we saw very little of the women too, who I guess were home looking after their husbands, and if we did see any, they were always friendly and polite.

Anyway, back to those loose ends, with the first one being the hash and opium. We needed somewhere better than the coach to store it, so our first stop was the only shop in town, to meet Sanjay, the owner. I'd been introduced to him the previous night at the bar, but like the rest of the evening, I couldn't remember him at all. He welcomed us with a smile, shaking our hands and offering us tea, which we graciously accepted.

In India, tea was like a sacred ritual, as the water was boiled and the leaves prepared. It then became an ancient ceremony, as the two were mixed and left to brew, which had to be timed precisely, so an egg timer-like instrument was used, with the sand falling from the top glass chamber to the bottom lasting exactly three minutes. All this had to be done before any business could be discussed; meanwhile, Gary performed another ancient ceremony: building a chillum.

Then the tea was poured, the chillum lit, and we finally got down to business, which like the tea preparation took time and was also slowed down by two other things: the chillum and that other ancient Eastern ritual, a lot of haggling. We went back and forth until finally a deal was struck that not only dealt with the hash and opium (we sold half of each to Sanjay and kept the rest for ourselves), it also took care of our accommodation needs too, because as part of the deal, Sanjay rented us rooms to stay in.

Another loose end was the coach, which had performed almost perfectly, thanks to John's efforts along the way. Only now, it was in need of a proper service on the engine, brakes, and steering. So our next call was to the only garage in Palolem, where hopefully the work could be done. It took a bit of haggling, but no tea and chillum this time before a price was agreed. So we now had somewhere to do the work and also a secure place to leave the coach for the duration of our stay.

So with that loose end tied up, we then headed for the only other business in the town, the bar, where we'd partied the night before and more of that local potent hooch.

29

Hub of the community: That's what the bar or pub is in most small towns and villages, no matter where you go in the world, and it seemed this was no different in paradise. I would have liked to think that living a simple life like these people did, there would be no need for strong alcohol or drugs, but that wasn't the case even here, where you could almost believe heaven on earth did exist because it was so beautiful. I found that out when we arrived and it turned into a party, which was mainly fuelled by the local potent hooch. So it seemed that even living in paradise wasn't enough, and like most other human beings on this planet, the people here also liked to abstract their reality any way they could, and we couldn't argue, as we were just the same. One of the main reasons we were on this journey was to sample all the mind-expanding substances we could find along the way.

As we entered the pub, Rashid, the bar's owner and producer of the local potent hooch (he also brewed a strange cloudy warm liquid he called beer), set up drinks for us, waving away all our attempts to reimbursing him, saying, "It's all on the house."

Then, with a smile, he knocked back a large belt of hooch himself, which made our attempts at drinking his fiery liquor look very tame, as all we could do was sip it. I didn't remember it being quite so potent from the night before, as this fiery-tasting liquid slowly burnt its way down my throat, setting my internal organs on fire. However, after sipping the first one, the second did start to go down easier, and by the third, well, that was enough for me, for the moment anyway, as it felt like my head was slowly being turned inside out. I had to sit down before I fell down. What I'd neglected to do that day was eat, which is why I think the hooch tasted so strong.

So once my head did start to clear, that was soon rectified by another of Rashid's concoctions and a local staple: fish curry. A more potent version was eaten by the fishermen and locals, but the steaming bowl of rice and fish that was put in front of me was supposed to be less spicy, more suited to the Western palette, but after it had cooled enough for me to eat, it made me feel like my internal organs were on fire again. I felt like I'd gone into nuclear meltdown, as my whole body started to pour with sweat. If this was supposed to be the mild curry, then Rashid's more potent one must have been like a full-on nuclear war to eat, but I was never adventurous enough to try it and find out.

However, let's go back to where the words *Western* and *palette* were mentioned, because they did trigger a memory from the party the night before, which was being introduced to some Western faces. Only like the rest of the night, when I woke up on the beach that morning, had been completely wiped from my memory banks. It was now, as I tried to recover from more hooch and the fish curry, I found they were real and not figments of my imagination. And where did we find them again? In the bar, of course.

There were nine of them, four guys and five girls, who like Gary had all dropped out and landed on this particular piece of heaven. They were all in their twenties and from various countries and backgrounds. However, they did have one thing in common: They never wanted to leave this beautiful place. This is where I should say that two of them, Kate and Tom, became part of the story too, because they had a direct influence over the next part of our journey, which I'll come to later. First, though, Gary had one last place to show us, and I promise you it's worth waiting for. Only now, our mode of transport would have to change, from a coach to a boat.

30

Butterfly Beach was a beautifully wild, isolated cove just north of Palolem. This was Gary's last gift to us on this journey, and it was like we'd reached the end of the rainbow and found the pot of gold. Only it wasn't gold in the form of money or coins; it was gold in the form of imagination, because like Palolem, it was another picture postcard piece of paradise. Only Butterfly Beach had an exclusivity to it, as it was only accessible by boat. So when I did step on to it for the first time, I felt like I was taking one giant leap for mankind. Not that we were walking on virgin ground for the first time, anyway, because Gary and our new friends had been there many times before. It just felt that little bit more special, because we had to make the extra effort to get there.

However, before we could set off to Butterfly Beach, which involved taking to the high seas, there was first the small matter of getting out of Rashid's bar sober enough to do so, and second securing a boat, of course. The second part was solved by the local fishermen, who hired us one of their boats. It was the sober part that would have to wait until another day, because to secure the deal for the boat involved the consumption of a lot more hooch (and another day/night being wiped from my memory bank).

The second morning I woke up again on the beach, only this time, not with my face in the sand, and I did have some recollections of the previous night's activities, such as the boat deal and being introduced again to our roommates, who were staying at the same place as us. Then something I didn't remember, because now we were all going Butterfly Beach.

This gives me the chance to use the now-classic line from the movie, *Jaws*. Only I was using it before I'd heard it in Mr Spielberg's film: "We're going to need a bigger boat," as there were fourteen of us going now. One boat turned into two boats after we gathered up all the supplies we needed for the day, which required going back to Rashid's bar to get some of his nuclear curry and hooch to sustain us on our adventure. So with everything gathered and with the help of the fishermen, we split into two crews and were launched from the shore to make the half-mile journey.

This is where you're probably thinking that a bunch of spaced-out hippies, which is what we were, with no real boating experience was the perfect recipe for disaster. Well, I'm sorry to disappoint you, but there's no story of us all being swept out to sea, never to be seen again, or hitting a submerged rock and needing to abandon ship, because with the boys at the oars and the girls pointing the way, and a very favourable sea, we were soon making our final approach to wade in and touch down on Butterfly Beach.

31

Different, even though we'd only travelled just up the coast, Butterfly Beach was. The silvery sand still remained, but the tall sweeping palm trees that reached up the azure sky were gone, replaced by much shorter, denser foliage that encircled the beach, making it look like we'd landed in another country. For Don, John, Steve, and me, it was like we were conquering a new land; we spent the first part of the morning checking the place out. Not that it took that long, as you could walk from one end of the beach to other in about ten minutes. Even when you tried to go inland, the dense foliage made it impossible to go too far. What was still there, of course, was the Arabian Sea, and as we returned from our adventuring, Gary and the others were enjoying a swim.

I didn't think this picture of paradise that surrounded us could be improved on. Well, how wrong I was, because there before our very eyes, five beautiful young ladies were happily frolicking, naked, in the surf. What a sight it was, reminding me a little of Vondel Park back in the Dam during the summer, watching all those lovely Dutch ladies topping up their tans. Only now, the surroundings were almost as beautiful as the bodies that danced before us, and in the Dam, there was a certain amount of modesty, as the girls wore bikini bottoms. Here, caution, modesty, and every bit of clothing were thrown to the wind, as we all discarded our apparel and ran to join the frolicking. Not that I had many things to take off anyway, because by then, all my Western clothes were gone, mainly given away to people I met along the way or swapped for lighter Indian-style shirts and trousers, which were much more suitable for the hot climate.

We spent the rest of the morning playing in paradise, while the world beyond this place ceased to exist, for a few hours, anyway. It was another one of those moments in time where you'd like to get stuck forever, and the very thought that a paradise like this could become boring never entered my mind. However, like anywhere, even here that can happen.

It must have been midday by the time we were forced from our fun, because by then, the sun was overhead, and the cool morning Arabian Sea now felt like a hot bath. The sand on the beach had also become so hot, it was like you were walking on burning coals trying to get across it. So we retired to a cool shady spot out of the reach of those hot solar rays that took over to dominate the middle part of the day. Now it was time for some of Rashid's nuclear curry, washed down with more of his hooch, only before that, we all ate a piece of opium and smoked on one of Gary's chillums. It was the perfect combination to help float away the next few hours, all lost in our own drug-induced haze. This is how we spent the first part of the afternoon, until the sun moved well past its zenith, and the beach became bearable to walk on again.

Butterfly Beach also lived up to its name, because even at the hottest time of the day, while we sheltered from the blazing sun, you could see the most beautiful butterflies flitting from flower to flower, recharging their fuel cells with nature's own nuclear energy, sunshine and water, which created nectar. These creatures were the most brightly coloured things I'd ever seen in my life, so reminiscent of the country we were in. Now I could really understand why Gary and the others were so in love with this beautiful piece of coastline, because of its hidden treasures. Butterfly and Palolem beaches were still mostly unspoiled, because tourism hadn't yet reached this part of Goa.

After the beach had cooled, it was back to the shore for more fun and frolics in the surf, which helped to sober us up before it was time to get back in the boats for a leisurely row back to Palolem. This was when an already perfect day was made complete, because after we arrived, instead of just disappearing into Rashid's bar, we sat under one of those tall palm trees on the beach to witness another one of nature's truly spectacular events: the sun going down. Every day was unique in its own particular way, as the colour of the sky and clouds went through yellow, orange, red, and purple to black, with even some blues and greys thrown in for contrast. That was then replaced by the largest silvery moon I'd ever seen in my life, casting a magical spell as it created glittering patterns over the wine-dark Arabian Sea.

This was the first of many late afternoons/early evenings watching nature's own widescreen TV, as there was little else to do anyway. It was the perfect way to round off any day we spent at Butterfly Beach.

32

Christmas is the great Western winter festival of consumerism; once you pass a certain age, it becomes more of a pain than pleasure. The holiday was almost upon us, which I'm sure would have been unnoticed here in paradise, if it didn't precede the real thing to celebrate at this time: the new year. All my life, I could remember celebrating both these events in Bournemouth, surrounded by family and friends, going through the same routine of buying boring presents, enforced merriment, and too much booze and turkey on the big day. We only realised it was coming up because of talk in Rashid's bar about the plans the people of Palolem had to celebrate the new year. They were mainly of the Hindu religion but knew of this Western thing we call Christmas, but it was the new year that was their celebration. It was very impressive for a small town in the middle of nowhere.

But this year was going to be different for me, unless I headed back to Bombay to get a flight home, but the thought of doing that never came close to entering my head. It seemed the farther I got away from northern Europe, the less I wanted to go back, especially now, as it was the middle of winter there. If I was going anywhere from here, it would have to be farther south or east into this amazing country.

First, though, there was the small matter of Christmas Day to contend with, and we planned to spend it on Butterfly Beach. Only after a little too much merriment in Rashid's bar on Christmas Eve, it felt safer to spend it on Palolem Beach instead, doing the same thing as we'd do on Butterfly Beach: as little as humanly possible, only without the extra effort of rowing a boat.

Who would have thought back in May, when we set off from Bournemouth, that in a little over six months, we'd be spending Christmas Day in paradise. It was like a dream come true and the best Christmas present I'd ever had in my life.

The days between Christmas Day and New Year's Eve were spent doing pretty much the same: just sunning ourselves on the beach or having a cooling swim in the Arabian Sea, all intertwined, of course, with drinking in Rashid's bar. The people of Palolem went about their preparations for what was the biggest night of the year for them, and for us too, I guess. Only it all felt so different under a scorching sun, instead of freezing your n*ts off back in Blighty.

By the time the actual day did arrive, there was such a buzz around the town that by midday, as we lay on the beach, we could hear the snap, crackle, and pop of firecrackers being let off in town. It must have gone on for at least two hours, until it got a point where it almost sounded like a war zone, so many were going off. Then all at once, the whole place went quiet, as if someone had pulled a plug from the wall. Now there was an ominous silence as everybody waited for the sun to go down and for the real fireworks to begin.

Before it did all start, I had no idea just how crazy the Indian people were for pyrotechnics. Even before it had gone completely dark, for the next six hours, every home in the town put on its own amazing display. We just sat outside Rashid's bar, drinking hooch and smoking more of Gary's chillums, watching display after display, wondering if they were ever going to end. It truly was one of the most memorable and spectacular nights we spent there, and what a way to welcome in the year of 1977. Once we were into it, it wasn't long before things did start to change, which is summed up by the opening words of the next chapter.

33

Paradise Lost: Could it ever be? I guess the answer is yes, because it was about to happen to two of us from our close-knit group of idlers whose only pursuit for over four weeks had been to do as little as possible. For me personally, I don't think I'd ever spent this much time just lazing around. There were, of course, the four weeks I'd spent in a Swiss prison, fighting for my freedom the previous year, but I felt that didn't count, as it was forced upon me, and I couldn't relax anyway. Here, where there were no locked doors, or the threat of ten years in prison hanging over my head, life was like a permanent holiday. One day drifted into another, with the only real decision we had to make being whether to spend the day on Butterfly Beach.

However, just when you think all is right with the world and nothing really can go wrong, that's usually when life comes to bite you on the ass, because now sex raised its ugly head (excuse the pun). Not that sex wasn't something I'm sure we all were thinking about, especially after seeing those frolicking naked females on Butterfly Beach, only they were all spoken for by Gary and the four guys already here. There were local girls, but as Gary said, "Go near one of those, and you'll more than likely find a shotgun up your arse, or have wedding bells ringing in your ears. Whichever way, it was best to stay away from them."

What we needed was a brothel in Palolem to service those needs, only in such a small place, there wasn't much call for one, because we'd probably be its only customers. There was one other possibility, which was to drive back to Panaji to Pan's place. The problem with that, though, was the coach was out of action, awaiting new brake linings, which had been ordered. Only like everything else in India, they would take a long time to arrive. This meant the only transport available to us was an old truck the garage owner had, which looked like it was held together with string and chewing gum, like most other Indian vehicles. The truck was mainly used by Sanjay, the shop owner, and Rashid, the bar owner, to bring in fresh supplies from Panaji once a week.

So it looked like any sexual activity on Don's, John's, Steve's, or my part was going to have to wait for the moment, which didn't seem to be a problem, except for Steve; ever since I'd know him, he could never keep his hands to himself for very long and was always on the lookout for a fine young filly. He now became the catalyst that would bring an end to our idyllic lifestyle here in paradise. Not only did he get caught with his pants down and his cock in Kate, one of our fellow idlers, one dark night on the beach by her boyfriend Tom, who'd gone looking for her, he also admitted that he'd been having his wicked way with one of Rashid's daughters when Kate wasn't available.

All this was right under our noses. I knew he could be a devious SOB at times, but he'd really outdone himself this time; his dalliance with Kate was understandable, as she was quite attractive and flirty. We all wanted to get to know her better, after seeing her frolicking naked in the surf on Butterfly Beach, only as we were newcomers to this heavenly haven, some self-control was called for, so as not to ruin a perfect situation.

Tom didn't make too much fuss about what happened, not wanting to add fuel to any fire that was already burning. However, it wasn't Tom we had to worry about. The problem now was obviously making sure Rashid remained unaware of Steve's dalliance with his daughter, which after what Gary said about not getting involved with the local girls could affect all of us who wanted to stay here in Palolem. Only when it came to sex, Steve wasn't thinking about us or with his head. No, all the thinking was going on in his pants.

34

Time is that inexorable thing we'd all like to turn back, only we know that's impossible. Well, this was a moment when a reverse time machine would have come in quite handy, because after considering all the possible ways of resolving the situation, we decided the best thing would be for Steve to move onwards and outwards. He could explore more of the country, and if his philandering ways with Rashid's daughter were discovered, he'd be long gone and all the other idlers left in Palolem could claim ignorance.

This was the moment when I would like to go back in time, so I could stop Steve before he started dipping his dick, because now, just when I was starting to enjoy doing nothing, and was quite happy to stay here in paradise, it seemed my time was up as well because he agreed it was a good idea to leave but didn't want to go alone. He asked me to join him, which under the circumstances I could hardly refuse, because if it wasn't for him, I wouldn't have been there in the first place.

Only it wasn't as simple as just packing our bags and leaving; there were some other issues to resolve before we could move on. The main one was what to do about our shares in the coach. So as a temporary measure, Don, John, and Gary agreed to buy our shares, and we could buy them back in early May, when the Magic Bus trail opened again. We planned to meet back up in Panaji, at Pan's place. The second part of this, of course, depended on us getting back in time; if we weren't there by the end of the first week in May, they would have to leave without us.

Once that was agreed, all that was left to do now was to leave Palolem without causing suspicion or letting on what we were up to (or rather what Steve had been into). So we went about our idling in the usual way over the next few days, which included one last visit to Butterfly Beach and, of course, hanging out at Rashid's bar in the evening. We mentioned the possibility of a boys and girls night out in Panaji sometime soon, which meant we needed transport to get there. So after those few days, it was back to the garage to hire the only transport available, that very dodgy-looking truck. During a test run around the town, it drove okay, even if it was very slowly, but at least it gave us some hope of getting to Panaji.

We spent our last night in Palolem doing nothing unusual, just drinking with the locals in Rashid's bar and then getting stoned on the beach and staring off into that endless starry sky. That sight never failed to fill you full of wonder, no matter how many times you'd seen it, and we'd done it many times since we'd been there. Only there was one difference this night, which of course was the prospect of Steve and me getting back on the road again, which was now starting to fill me with anticipation that only new adventure can bring. All the thoughts I had before of wanting to stay were long gone from my mind.

Our conversation did come around to what we were going to do next, only the drink and drugs started to take their effect, so it didn't get very far. There would be plenty of time to think and talk about that when we got to Panaji the following day, which was where we planned to have our last real party together. The rest of our last night in Palolem was left to astral-projecting through the star-filled Milky

Way, laid out before our eyes, and wishing on the occasional falling star. It truly was the perfect way to end a perfect stay, feeling like the proverbial grain of sand on this paradisiacal beach, lost in the vastness of this wondrous universe.

When we awoke the following morning, it was back to the reality of getting out of Palolem, which we managed to do without too much fuss. There were just a few friendly faces there at the garage to wave us off, which included Rashid and his daughter, who Steve had done the dirty with, but thankfully, there were no tears, just smiles and the wish of a safe return journey. The first leg went surprisingly well, once we got off the spooky side road, with all its strange noises that took you to Palolem, and back on the main highway.

The truck's old diesel engine could get up some speed, so we were soon closing in on our destination. When we did get to Pan's place, we were treated to a repeat performance of our first few nights there; Pan and his staff again tended to our every need. There wasn't quite the same exuberance as then, because that night, we still had the momentum from being on the road and the prospect of paradise waiting at Butterfly Beach.

Whereas this night marked the end to Steve and I idling and the somewhat unexpected beginning of the next part of our adventure. So there was a certain amount of sadness tinged to the evening, because after being together for over two months, our group of idlers had become very close. Even if Steve, Kate, and Tom weren't quite so close now, after what had happened between them, at least they were still talking to each other.

However, as the festivities wore on into the night, the sadness and hostilities disappeared completely, as the drugs took over, and the topic of conversation came round to where Steve and I were actually going next.

35

Sri Lanka was formally known as Ceylon. The island was a short ferry ride away at the very bottom tip of mainland India. I'd always associated the name with tea, because it seemed to be on every tea packet I'd ever read. It was a place Gary mentioned during the conversation that evening. He went there during his first visit to the India and ended up in Galle, a small town on the most southerly tip of the island. According to him, it was another tropical paradise just waiting to be explored and rivalled the beauty of Palolem and Butterfly Beach. He also reckoned we could easily reach it with plenty of time to spare, so we'd have at least six weeks to enjoy the place before we needed to be back here in time to rendezvous with Don, John, and Gary for the start of the new Magic Bus season.

Out of all the places that were mentioned over the evening, it did catch my imagination and would mean, by the time we got there, we would have travelled the whole length of the country, which still left half the continent to go, so there was still plenty of India left to see along the way.

There was also the small matter of how we were going to get there; now we'd lost the comfort of the coach, we'd have to start using India's public transport system, an experience that really was like travelling back in time, because the trains we were about to ride on were mostly driven by steam, something that had long disappeared back in the UK.

First, though, before we did set off on the next part of this journey, there was the rest of the party to enjoy, which was driven mainly by Colombian cocaine. We ended up all moving to the nearby beach to watch the sunrise. It was something to really remember our last night together by, because it was almost as spectacular as watching the sunset on Palolem Beach. This glow of light gradually lit up the sky over the city and jungle, and then the first rays of sunlight caught the clouds and cut through them before burning the clouds away completely, almost like watching a giant Venetian blind being opened, with the colours going in reverse to a sunset, from black through purple, red, orange, and yellow, ending up in bright blue.

When the daylight was complete, we took our last dip together in the Arabian Sea, and when the sun got too hot, we headed back to the bathhouse under the café, where we spent the rest of that day and most of the following night having all our other needs taken care of. Well, Don, John, Steve, and me, that is, while the others took care of themselves.

This is probably a good time to introduce our other fellow idlers, before we do go our separate ways. They had become an integral part of our lives over the last two months, so I think they deserve a mention. I've already mentioned Kate and Tom, because of Steve's philandering. There was also Kate's friend Claire; they were both from London, got on a Magic Bus about five years ago looking for adventure, and had been lost in India ever since. They kind of reminded me of Liza and Lucy, who'd been with us on our journey until we got to Ahmadabad, and I had the pleasure of making their full acquaintance.

Next came Anna from Hanover in Germany, Helena from Rotterdam in Holland, and Susan from Toronto. They all met in Panaji and then found their way to Palolem by word of mouth.

Tom originated from Kansas in the USA. He like Gary had been coming back to this beautiful place for many years now.

Next came Paul from Bristol in the UK, who liked to think of himself as a professional idler, having spent a lot of years developing it to a fine art lying on Palolem and Butterfly Beach.

Serge was from just outside of Paris in France, and last but not least was Raf, who was of Colombian descent. They were the most recent additions to this happy bunch; they'd been in India for almost three years now and had decided to stay as long as possible. Raf had a particular liking for his country's most famous exported product, as he hoovered up loads of the stuff during our last party together.

So as our second morning in Panaji broke, there was only one thing left to do now, and the real reason we were there anyway, which was for the rest of the idlers to head back to Palolem, while dropping Steve and I at Panaji's Kamali Station to catch our train. Many hugs were shared, goodbyes were said, and even a few tears were shed. We waved the truck on its way and then decided which way we were actually going to go on the next leg of this adventure.

36

British Rail, that much maligned but essential part of the UK's public transport system, was something I'd ridden many times in the past. Like I said, it did have its problems. However, it was never going to be the same again after the experience I was about to have, because the Indian railway system was a whole different ball game compared to it. Just walking into Kamali Station was more like entering a marketplace than a train station. It also smelled like one too, with all the livestock and animals that were there. Chickens, goats, even a cow, and they were just the ones I could see. Who knows what was lurking in the covered cages some of the people were travelling with? And some of these people looked like they should be in cages themselves, they appeared so untamed and wild.

It certainly was a very interesting first impression and one that made us both hesitate before heading for the ticket office, which was an adventure in itself. When we did manage to wade through the crowd of people and animals to stand in front of the sales clerk, we faced our next decision: Where we were actually going? I know we'd talked about Sri Lanka, but what we hadn't bargained for was how long we'd have to wait for a train to take us there. The Indian rail system was big, as it covered the whole country, but the trains were overcrowded and unreliable. That in the end would determine where we went. So we left it to fate and asked these questions: Which direction was the next train due at the station going, and were there tickets available?

Well, the answer to the first, it seemed, was that fate was with us, because the next train was going south, and the answer to the second was superfluous, because there were always tickets available. This is where the overcrowding part came in too, because if there weren't seats available in the carriages, then you simply clambered up onto the roof or found anywhere you could hang on or sit until the next station, where everything changed again. As then people got on and off, so you could reposition yourself to a more comfortable spot.

So we both bought open travel cards dated for when we were due back in Panaji, as they weren't expensive, and it would make it easier for any future travel, because they covered buses as well. Then we fought our way through a sea of potential passengers towards the platform, to find somewhere to sit to wait for the train. I kept thinking there was little chance we'd get on the train; there were so many people waiting.

When the train did arrive about an hour later, it was like a giant hissing, wheezing monster as it entered the station in a torrent steam and noise. It looked like a 1940s steam train, not that I knew how old it actually was, but it was something that had long disappeared back in the UK. Only now, it seemed, they were still going strong in this part of the world, as all the trains we travelled on out there were steam-driven. It was almost like a childhood dream for me, as I'd always wanted to ride on one, but they'd all gone out of service before I started travelling by train. India had some modern trains, only not in this part of the country.

Next came the small matter of getting on the thing, and I realised just how popular Panaji was, because it was like this tidal wave of passengers getting off the train. It looked like most of them on it got off and were hit by an immovable force of passengers wanting to get on. So the battle commenced, and Steve and I were lucky to be at the side of the main tussle, which was in the centre. We just watched as it slowly became like a dance. The people getting on and off realised that unless they started giving way to each other, nobody was going anywhere. So they started weaving through and around one another, with their bags on their heads and animals or cages in tow; it took on a real surreal quality, as they bobbed and weaved amongst each other.

In the end, it must have taken almost hour before the whole changeover was complete, with everybody who wanted to be on the train settled somewhere. Steve and I were lucky, because we ended up on the roof of the third carriage from the front of the train. I say lucky, because not only did we get a fantastic panoramic view of countryside we were passing through, but also the lovely cool air (avoiding the bugs, that is) kept us well ventilated once we did get moving. We weren't stuck in one of the smelly, stuffy carriages surrounded by sweaty people, chickens, goats, and Mildred the cow. It seemed to me that in India, cows (who were sacred to most of the people there), goats, and chickens travelled in better style than most people, who, like Steve and me, were clinging to the roof.

37

On safari, hunting big game: That's what it felt like as we rode the roof of the train watching India flow by (without the guns and killing, that is). We cut through what felt like endless jungles of tall palm trees that would then open up into large savannahs of grassy plains, where we would spot occasional elephant in watering holes. That's what I meant about the safari bit, before disappearing back again into more palm trees and jungle.

We then settled into the next leg of what had turned into an even bigger adventure. After only a few hours, Palolem and Butterfly Beach had disappeared in both memory and proximity. Our first stop was Mangalore; its name conjured up all sorts of strange macabre images in my head, from the *mangle* part, that is. Only names and imagination can be misleading, because when we finally arrived there, viewing it from our lofty position atop of the train, it didn't look that different from most other Indian cities I'd seen so far on this journey, with its mix of both poor and rich areas, all in close proximity.

This was where we had to make our second decision on the direction we were going, as the train we were on was about to turn east to go inland towards Bangalore. We needed to decide whether to go with it, or stay on the rail line running south down the coast. Only to do that would mean an overnight stay in Mangalore, as the next train going south, wasn't leaving until the following morning. So we consulted the train map and talked to the rail staff, although that was mainly done in sign language, due to their lack of English and our lack of whatever dialect they were speaking. That was another thing about India; in just one city alone, there could be three or four different dialects spoken.

Anyway, back to the decision, which was really made for us, because if we were going to Sri Lanka, it made more sense to stay on the coast until we got to Shoranur and then turned east and headed towards Madurai and Rameswaram, where there was a ferry to Sri Lanka.

Galle became our focus, because after spending over two months in Palolem, enjoying just lying on the beach, doing as little as possible, the prospect of more of that sounded very attractive. We found a hotel for the night not far from the station, so we could head off early the following morning and gather up supplies of food and water for the next part of the journey (there wasn't exactly a buffet car on the train to get supplies from). Only to do this meant a foray into Mangalore, which wasn't scary at all, reminding me a bit of Ahmadabad, because like then, we were surrounded by begging kids. That done, it was back to the hotel to get a good rest, as we had no idea when our next decent night's sleep would be.

The station was busy when we returned the following morning, with it looking like the same farmyard/marketplace we'd seen at Panaji. Only now, after watching the previous day's fight/dance between passengers and animals getting on and off the train, when the train arrived, we decided to stake an even better place on one of the carriage roofs. We had enjoyed the experience of being up there the previous day. This is how we spent all our train rides for the rest of the journey to Sri Lanka, and even after we got there. It really was the best way to see all the sights passing by, as we sat back-to-back for support, pointing out things we might have missed if we'd been inside the carriage.

To some extent, we did miss travelling in the coach, which gave us more freedom, as there were more roads to explore, rather than just one track. There was also the flexibility the coach gave us to travel when we wanted, with no timetable. The trains rarely ran on time, and of course the coach was more comfortable. However, it wouldn't have afforded us this fantastic panoramic view, which I'll mention one last time.

The other thing that simplified our lives now was, we were back to just the two of us, so considering other people's needs was no longer a part of our lives. As we closed in on Rameshwaram to catch the ferry, all we had to do was think about ourselves and what we were going to do once we reached Galle.

38

Sri Lanka again, only I didn't have to use my imagination to visualise it. We were seeing it for real as we crossed the Palk Strait between the mainland and the island. The island was a tropical paradise where dreams were made and fantasies came true; that's how one tourist brochure I saw described the place.

First, though, a little bit about Sri Lanka's past and present, because as an outsider seeing the place for the first time, you couldn't help but be overwhelmed by its beauty. But when you scratch the surface of a place that's as beautiful as this, you'll always find a much darker story, no matter what the tourist brochure says; it was like India in that way, as it gave you a false impression with all its peace and natural beauty. Underneath that façade lay a long history of bloodshed between the two largest ethnic groups on the island, the Tamils and the Sinhalese, which had been brewing for almost a century before civil war finally broke out in July 1983. This didn't affect us while we were there, so I won't go into further detail.

For us, it was another glorious train ride down the west coast of the island, passing through Wilpaththu National Park, which again gave us the feel of being on safari, as we spotted more wildlife from the roof of the carriage. After crossing from India, the Arabian Sea, which had been to our right, had changed to the Indian Ocean. We stopped briefly in Colombo, the island's commercial capital, for fresh supplies of food and water, before heading on to our final destination Galle.

Once we got there and went through the town to the beach, it was just how Gary described it: another picture-perfect paradise. I know I used that phrase earlier to sum up Palolem and Butterfly Beach, but I have to use those words again, because that's the only way to do it justice.

Somehow, I'd got it into my head from what Gary said that we'd have the place to ourselves, so it came as a complete surprise when we found all these Aussie and Kiwi surfers there, about forty men and women in their twenties. We found out later they'd been coming here for years; the angle of the shoreline and gradient of the beach created particularly good surfing waves.

So now, instead of kicking back and relaxing like we planned to do, it was the opposite, as we became the centre of attention as the token Poms, which is what they liked to call us. And we got invited to join in all their fun. I have to say it started off well, as I'd never imagined myself surfing before. It was only something I'd seen on TV until now. Our days were spent like they were on Butterfly Beach, only instead of swimming or splashing around, we learnt how to surf. Once you got the hang of it after a few days, it really was a lot of fun. During the morning, we'd go surfing, and then when it got too hot, we'd head for the shade and chill, getting stoned until the late afternoon. Then, we'd go surfing again, and the evenings.

Well, what else would you expect a load of young Aussie and Kiwis to do? Party, of course, sometimes going into Galle to drink at a local bar, while other times building a fire on the beach and having their own private parties. It did get rather raunchy once the booze started to flow, almost bordering on an orgy; both Steve and I were more than welcome to join in, getting lucky on too many occasions to mention. This became the pattern of our lives for the next month; it was even better than the paradise we found at Butterfly Beach, because there was sex here too. Out of all the paradises we did find that summer/winter, this last one had to be the best. I'm sure that lured me into a false sense of security, because I certainly wasn't ready for what happened next.

39

Paradise was lost again, which unlike before, when we had to leave Palolem because of Steve's philandering, really was over this time. After coming round bleary-eyed from another night of unbridled sex and booze on the beach, I discovered my document belt was gone. Talk about being sober instantly, because my whole life depended on that belt. Money, passport, and travel pass were gone. Without it, I had nothing. Then Steve showed up, saying his was gone too, which made us wonder what the f★★k was going on. The rest of that morning was spent frantically searching the area where we'd partied the previous night, only being very drunk for most of it, who knows where we went? Could we have buried them amongst the palm trees like before, when we went to surf? We checked out where we normally did this but came up empty too.

Now we were really freaking out, trying to think of any other places we might have used to hide the belts, but nothing came to mind. By then, some of our Aussie and Kiwi friends became aware of our situation and offered to help search. But as we looked around at enormity of the task, we could have spent the rest of our lives digging around on that beach, never to find anything again. Only we weren't giving up that easily, and I wish I could say here that our belts were found, but after spending all morning and some of the afternoon looking and digging, nothing showed up.

So now, we tried not to think our world was crashing down around us; the only other explanation was that someone had stolen our belts. We had little alternative than to head into Galle and report them missing to the local police. They were very understanding of our situation but couldn't really do anything about it, apart from issue us letters confirming the loss of our money and documents. They explained why we would need the letters, because since we had no passports, we had to go to the British embassy in Colombo to get new ones. That added another complication to it all; how were we going to get to Colombo without any money? The police had the answer to that too, because now we didn't a passport, they wouldn't allow us to stay in Galle, as it was illegal to travel abroad without one.

That meant we'd have to stay overnight at the police station and then be accompanied by a cop the following day to the train station, where he would explain our situation to the rail staff, who would hopefully let us travel free (thankfully, they did). Only that wasn't the worst part that waited for us when we got to the embassy, because when we did, we hit the mind f**k of British bureaucracy and its Catch-22: The staff refused to issue us new passports because we had no form of identity. So as we tried to explain for more than the hundredth time, how could we do that when we'd loss all our documents? Instead, they would only issue us repatriation letters and pay for our flights back to the UK, which we'd have to pay back later, because the money to do this was only a loan.

This was when our world did finally crash down to the ground, because we couldn't even go back to the beach in Galle to say goodbye, let alone back to Panaji to meet up with Don, John, and

Gary like we planned. We were now at the mercy of the British authorities, who wouldn't even let us leave the embassy until we were due at the airport to get our flight.

So for the second time on this journey, I found myself incarcerated, only now, it was at the hands of the British. It wasn't as serious as when I was in Switzerland, but I still didn't like having my liberty taken away from me. I just hoped the reason for my stay in that Swiss jail didn't come to the attention of my new captors and complicate thing even more, which thankfully, it didn't.

It couldn't have been more than three days between us losing our documents until we were sitting on the plane waiting to take off, which all went by in a bureaucratic blur. As the plane taxied out onto the runway to take off, it was another first for me that year; I'd never flown before. It all happened so fast, I was in a complete daze and never really had time to consider that our journey was now actually ending.

However, the one thing that did jolt me out of my stupefied state was the plane actually taking off. First, feeling the acceleration as we headed down the runway, then when the wheels did leave the ground, the exhilaration and the feeling of being weightless for the first time. This was something I've never gotten used to, and it always takes me back to the first time I felt it.

As the plane rose up into the sky, we witnessed Sri Lanka in all its glory as it appeared in the window, which only made me want to go back, but that wasn't under my control now. All I could really feel was sadness that this journey was ending. It wasn't until later into the flight that I started to feel a certain amount of anticipation that we were going home. However, there was one last irony on this return flight, which was the plane making a stopover, and where do you think that would be. Switzerland, of course.

40

Triumphant return; now that has a ring to it, and if there had been a proper plan to start with, that's how I would have wanted it to end, or even prodigal son returns home with riches from a distant land. That has a ring to it too. That also wasn't to be, because the word that does spring to mind, which is much more appropriate, is *ignominious*. That's how it really felt after such an amazing adventure to now find myself back at the home I'd grown up in, staying with my parents.

It certainly wasn't the way I wanted it to finish, only I had no idea how it would end when we set off almost exactly a year to the day from small-town Bournemouth. Now finding myself with only the Indian clothes I was standing in and without a penny to my name, owing the government four hundred pounds for my flight home plus another fifty pounds once I was here for bureaucracy charges and to get home from Heathrow Airport. With no way of paying them back, you can imagine how I felt as I sat my old room, staring at this stranger reflected in the mirror.

So as I get to end of this story, I'd like to focus on the positive, because so much did come from what I'd seen and been through in such a short space of time. It felt like I'd lived a whole lifetime in just one year; I had done more than some people do in their whole life. Now as I tried to pick up the pieces of the life I once knew, I was seeing it through very different eyes, a life that now seemed so meaningless to me. After my world, horizons and mind had been so expanded, I tried to come to terms with being back in a small town and what had happened over that year. It made me feel like I never did really come back completely, which I guess is probably right, because parts of me had been left on the many roads I'd travelled. I was a very different person.

However, the most positive thing that really did change my life forever was the original artwork I started to create when I was in the Dam, which has led me on to creating some amazing and beautiful pictures. I never would have had the courage to try before I went on this journey; I'm still creating those pictures today and plan to keep doing it until I'm incapable of lifting a brush, pen, mouse, or whatever way I'm working by then

So now, I'll try to find the words to sum up this whole experience. l can only think that even if it did end in an inglorious way, after such a tumultuous journey, which took me to places I never imagined travelling to, and meet people that still remain fond in my memory. And of course thank Steve for taking me on this journey in the first place.

I will always be rich in the memories captured in these words. They will always define my life in every way.